MznLnx

Missing Links Exam Preps

Exam Prep for

Intermediate Algebra

Aufmann, Barker, Lockwood, 6th Edition

The MznLnx Exam Prep is your link from the texbook and lecture to your exams.
The MznLnx Exam Preps are unauthorized and comprehensive reviews of your textbooks.

All material provided by MznLnx and Rico Publications (c) 2010
Textbook publishers and textbook authors do not particpate in or contribute to these reviews.

MznLnx

Rico
Publications

Exam Prep for Intermediate Algebra
6th Edition
Aufmann, Barker, Lockwood

Publisher: Raymond Houge
Assistant Editor: Michael Rouger
Text and Cover Designer: Lisa Buckner
Marketing Manager: Sara Swagger
Project Manager, Editorial Production: Jerry Emerson
Art Director: Vernon Lowerui

Product Manager: Dave Mason
Editorial Assitant: Rachel Guzmanji
Pedagogy: Debra Long
Cover Image: Jim Reed/Getty Images
Text and Cover Printer: City Printing, Inc.
Compositor: Media Mix, Inc.

(c) 2010 Rico Publications
ALL RIGHTS RESERVED. No part of this work covered by the copyright may be reproduced or used in any form or by an means--graphic, electronic, or mechanical, including photocopying, recording, taping, Web distribution, information storage, and retrieval systems, or in any other manner--without the written permission of the publisher.

For more information about our products, contact us at:

Dave.Mason@RicoPublications.com

For permission to use material from this text or

product, submit a request online to:

Dave.Mason@RicoPublications.com

Printed in the United States
ISBN:

Contents

CHAPTER 1
Review of Real Numbers — 1

CHAPTER 2
First-Degree Equations and Inequalities — 15

CHAPTER 3
Linear Functions and Inequalities in Two Variables — 29

CHAPTER 4
Systems of Equations and Inequalities — 46

CHAPTER 5
Polynomials and Exponents — 58

CHAPTER 6
Rational Expressions — 76

CHAPTER 7
Rational Exponents and Radicals — 91

CHAPTER 8
Quadratic Equations and Inequalities — 105

CHAPTER 9
Functions and Relations — 121

CHAPTER 10
Exponential and Logarithmic Functions — 131

CHAPTER 11
Sequences and Series — 136

CHAPTER 12
Conic sections — 141

ANSWER KEY — 144

TO THE STUDENT

COMPREHENSIVE

The *MznLnx* Exam Prep series is designed to help you pass your exams. Editors at MznLnx review your textbooks and then prepare these practice exams to help you master the textbook material. Unlike study guides, workbooks, and practice tests provided by the texbook publisher and textbook authors, *MznLnx* gives you **all** of the material in each chapter in exam form, not just samples, so you can be sure to nail your exam.

MECHANICAL

The MznLnx Exam Prep series creates exams that will help you learn the subject matter as well as test you on your understanding. Each question is designed to help you master the concept. Just working through the exams, you gain an understanding of the subject--its a simple mechanical process that produces success.

INTEGRATED STUDY GUIDE AND REVIEW

MznLnx is not just a set of exams designed to test you, its also a comprehensive review of the subject content. Each exam question is also a review of the concept, making sure that you will get the answer correct without having to go to other sources of material. You learn as you go! Its the easiest way to pass an exam.

HUMOR

Studying can be tedious and dry. MznLnx's instructional design includes moderate humor within the exam questions on occassion, to break the tedium and revitalize the brain

Chapter 1. Review of Real Numbers 1

1. In geometry, two lines or planes if one falls on the other in such a way as to create congruent adjacent angles. The term may be used as a noun or adjective. Thus, referring to Figure 1, the line AB is the _____ to CD through the point B.
    a. Thing
    b. Perpendicular0
    c. Undefined
    d. Undefined

2. In geometry, a _____ is defined as a quadrilateral where all four of its angles are right angles.
    a. Rectangle0
    b. Thing
    c. Undefined
    d. Undefined

3. An _____ or member of a set is an object that when collected together make up the set.
    a. Element0
    b. Thing
    c. Undefined
    d. Undefined

4. In mathematics, the _____ , or members of a set or more generally a class are all those objects which when collected together make up the set or class.
    a. Thing
    b. Elements0
    c. Undefined
    d. Undefined

5. The _____ of a ring R is defined to be the smallest positive integer n such that n a = 0, for all a in R.
    a. Thing
    b. Characteristic0
    c. Undefined
    d. Undefined

6. _____ is a natural number that has exactly two distinct natural number divisors, which are 1 and the _____ itself.
    a. Prime number0
    b. Thing
    c. Undefined
    d. Undefined

7. In mathematics, a _____ can mean either an element of the set {1, 2, 3, ...} (i.e the positive integers or the counting numbers) or an element of the set {0, 1, 2, 3, ...} (i.e. the non-negative integers).
    a. Natural number0
    b. Thing
    c. Undefined
    d. Undefined

8. In mathematics, a _____ number (or a _____) is a natural number that has exactly two (distinct) natural number divisors, which are 1 and the _____ number itself.
    a. Prime0
    b. Thing
    c. Undefined
    d. Undefined

9. A _____ number is a positive integer which has a positive divisor other than one or itself.
    a. Thing
    b. Composite0
    c. Undefined
    d. Undefined

10. In mathematics, an inequality is a statement about the relative size or order of two objects. For example 14 > 10, or 14 is _____ 10.
    a. Thing
    b. Greater than0
    c. Undefined
    d. Undefined

Chapter 1. Review of Real Numbers

11. _____, usually denoted symbolically by the Greek letter phi, Î¦, gives the location of a place on Earth north or south of the equator. _____ is an angular measurement in degrees (marked with Â°) ranging from 0Â° at the Equator (low _____) to 90Â° at the poles (90Â° N for the North Pole or 90Â° S for the South Pole; high _____). The complementary angle of a _____ is called the colatitude.
   a. Latitude0
   b. Thing
   c. Undefined
   d. Undefined

12. _____ is the fee paid on borrowed money.
   a. Interest0
   b. Thing
   c. Undefined
   d. Undefined

13. In mathematics, a _____ of an integer n, also called a factor of n, is an integer which evenly divides n without leaving a remainder.
   a. Divisor0
   b. Thing
   c. Undefined
   d. Undefined

14. In _____ algebra, a *-ring is an associative ring with an antilinear, antiautomorphism * : A ¨ A which is an involution.
   a. Thing
   b. Star0
   c. Undefined
   d. Undefined

15. In mathematics, an _____ number is a complex number whose square is a negative real number. They were defined in 1572 by Rafael Bombelli.
   a. Imaginary0
   b. Thing
   c. Undefined
   d. Undefined

16. A _____ is a number that is less than zero.
   a. Thing
   b. Negative number0
   c. Undefined
   d. Undefined

17. _____ is a set, with some particular properties and usually some additional structure, such as the operations of addition or multiplication, for instance.
   a. Thing
   b. Space0
   c. Undefined
   d. Undefined

18. In mathematics, a _____ can mean either an element of the set {1, 2, 3, ...} (i.e the positive integers) or an element of the set {0, 1, 2, 3, ...} (i.e. the non-negative integers).
   a. Whole number0
   b. Concept
   c. Undefined
   d. Undefined

19. The _____ are the only integral domain whose positive elements are well-ordered, and in which order is preserved by addition. Like the natural numbers, the _____ form a countably infinite set. The set of all _____ is usually denoted in mathematics by a boldface Z .
   a. Thing
   b. Integers0
   c. Undefined
   d. Undefined

20. In mathematics, _____ are essentially word problems that are designed to use mathematical critical thinking in everyday situations.
   a. Application problems0   b. Thing
   c. Undefined   d. Undefined

21. In mathematics, a _____ number is a number which can be expressed as a ratio of two integers. Non-integer _____ numbers (commonly called fractions) are usually written as the vulgar fraction a / b, where b is not zero.
   a. Rational0   b. Thing
   c. Undefined   d. Undefined

22. Mathematical _____ is used to represent ideas.
   a. Thing   b. Notation0
   c. Undefined   d. Undefined

23. A _____ is a numeral used to indicate a count. The most common use of the word today is to name the part of a fraction that tells the number or count of equal parts.
   a. Thing   b. Numerator0
   c. Undefined   d. Undefined

24. _____ is the writing of numbers in the base-ten numeral system, which uses various symbols called digits for ten distinct values 0, 1, 2, 3, 4, 5, 6, 7, 8 and 9 to represent numbers
   a. Thing   b. Decimal notation0
   c. Undefined   d. Undefined

25. A _____ is the part of a fraction that tells how many equal parts make up a whole, and which is used in the name of the fraction: "halves", "thirds", "fourths" or "quarters", "fifths" and so on.
   a. Denominator0   b. Concept
   c. Undefined   d. Undefined

26. A _____ decimal is a decimal fraction which ends after a definite number of digits.
   a. Terminating0   b. Thing
   c. Undefined   d. Undefined

27. A _____ is the part of the dividend that is left over when the dividend is not evenly divisible by the divisor.
   a. Thing   b. Remainder0
   c. Undefined   d. Undefined

28. A _____ decimal is a number whose decimal representation eventually becomes periodic (i.e. the same number sequence _____ indefinitely).
   a. Repeating0   b. Thing
   c. Undefined   d. Undefined

29. The _____ (symbol _____) and the millibar (symbol mbar, also mb) are units of pressure.
   a. Thing   b. Bar0
   c. Undefined   d. Undefined

Chapter 1. Review of Real Numbers

30. In mathematics, a _____ may be described informally as a number that can be given by an infinite decimal representation.
    a. Real number0
    b. Thing
    c. Undefined
    d. Undefined

31. In mathematics, an _____ number is any real number that is not a rational number- that is, it is a number which cannot be expressed as a fraction m/n, where m and n are integers.
    a. Thing
    b. Irrational0
    c. Undefined
    d. Undefined

32. In mathematics, an _____ is any real number that is not a rational number ¡ª that is, it is a number which cannot be expressed as m/n, where m and n are integers.
    a. Irrational number0
    b. Thing
    c. Undefined
    d. Undefined

33. In mathematics, _____ are any real number that is not a rational number ¡ª that is, it is a number which cannot be expressed as m/n, where m and n are integers.
    a. Irrational numbers0
    b. Thing
    c. Undefined
    d. Undefined

34. A _____ is a one-dimensional picture in which the integers are shown as specially-marked points evenly spaced on a line.
    a. Thing
    b. Number line0
    c. Undefined
    d. Undefined

35. The _____, the average in everyday English, which is also called the arithmetic _____ (and is distinguished from the geometric _____ or harmonic _____). The average is also called the sample _____. The expected value of a random variable, which is also called the population _____.
    a. Thing
    b. Mean0
    c. Undefined
    d. Undefined

36. A _____ is a symbolic representation denoting a quantity or expression. It often represents an "unknown" quantity that has the potential to change.
    a. Variable0
    b. Thing
    c. Undefined
    d. Undefined

37. In common philosophical language, a proposition or _____, is the content of an assertion, that is, it is true-or-false and defined by the meaning of a particular piece of language.
    a. Concept
    b. Statement0
    c. Undefined
    d. Undefined

38. In mathematics, the additive inverse, or _____ of a number n is the number that, when added to n, yields zero. The additive inverse of n is denoted −n. For example, 7 is −7, because 7 + (−7) = 0, and the additive inverse of −0.3 is 0.3, because −0.3 + 0.3 = 0.

a. Thing
b. Opposite0
c. Undefined
d. Undefined

39. In mathematics, the _____ of a number n is the number that, when added to n, yields zero. The _____ of n is denoted −n. For example, 7 is −7, because 7 + (−7) = 0, and the _____ of −0.3 is 0.3, because −0.3 + 0.3 = 0.
    a. Thing
    b. Additive inverse0
    c. Undefined
    d. Undefined

40. In mathematics, the _____ inverse, or opposite, of a number n is the number that, when added to n, yields zero. The _____ inverse of n is denoted −n.
    a. Thing
    b. Additive0
    c. Undefined
    d. Undefined

41. A _____ is a function that assigns a number to subsets of a given set.
    a. Measure0
    b. Thing
    c. Undefined
    d. Undefined

42. _____ element of an element x with respect to a binary operation * with identity element e is an element y such that x * y = y * x = e. In particular,
    a. Thing
    b. Inverse0
    c. Undefined
    d. Undefined

43. In mathematics, the _____ (or modulus) of a real number is its numerical value without regard to its sign.
    a. Thing
    b. Absolute value0
    c. Undefined
    d. Undefined

44. In mathematics, an _____ is a statement about the relative size or order of two objects.
    a. Thing
    b. Inequality0
    c. Undefined
    d. Undefined

45. An _____ is a combination of numbers, operators, grouping symbols and/or free variables and bound variables arranged in a meaningful way which can be evaluated..
    a. Thing
    b. Expression0
    c. Undefined
    d. Undefined

46. _____ is the state of being greater than any finite real or natural number, however large.
    a. Infinite0
    b. Thing
    c. Undefined
    d. Undefined

47. In set theory, an _____ is a set that is not a finite set. Infinite sets may be countable or uncountable.
    a. Infinite set0
    b. Thing
    c. Undefined
    d. Undefined

48. In set theory, _____ are such that are not finite sets.

a. Concept
b. Infinite sets
c. Undefined
d. Undefined

49. In mathematics, a set is called _____ if there is a bijection between the set and some set of the form {1, 2, ..., n} where n is a natural number.
   a. Finite
   b. Thing
   c. Undefined
   d. Undefined

50. In mathematics, a _____ occurs if there is a bijection between the set and some set of the form 1, 2, ..., n where n is a natural number.
   a. Concept
   b. Finite set
   c. Undefined
   d. Undefined

51. In mathematics and more specifically set theory, the _____ set is the unique set which contains no elements.
   a. Thing
   b. Empty
   c. Undefined
   d. Undefined

52. In measure theory, a _____ is a set that is negligible for the purposes of the measure in question.
   a. Null set
   b. Concept
   c. Undefined
   d. Undefined

53. In mathematics, _____ is an elementary arithmetic operation. When one of the numbers is a whole number, _____ is the repeated sum of the other number.
   a. Multiplication
   b. Thing
   c. Undefined
   d. Undefined

54. In set theory and other branches of mathematics, the _____ of a collection of sets is the set that contains everything that belongs to any of the sets, but nothing else.
   a. Thing
   b. Union
   c. Undefined
   d. Undefined

55. In mathematics, the _____ of two sets A and B is the set that contains all elements of A that also belong to B (or equivalently, all elements of B that also belong to A), but no other elements.
   a. Intersection
   b. Thing
   c. Undefined
   d. Undefined

56. In elementary algebra, an _____ is a set that contains every real number between two indicated numbers and may contain the two numbers themselves.
   a. Thing
   b. Interval
   c. Undefined
   d. Undefined

57. _____ is the notation in which permitted values for a variable are expressed as ranging over a certain interval; "5 < x < 9" is an example of the application of _____.
   a. Interval notation
   b. Thing
   c. Undefined
   d. Undefined

Chapter 1. Review of Real Numbers

58. In geometry, an _____ is a point at which a line segment or ray terminates.
    a. Endpoint0
    b. Thing
    c. Undefined
    d. Undefined

59. _____ is a mathematical notation for describing a set by stating the properties that its members must satisfy.
    a. Thing
    b. Set-builder notation0
    c. Undefined
    d. Undefined

60. A _____ of a number is the product of that number with any integer.
    a. Thing
    b. Multiple0
    c. Undefined
    d. Undefined

61. _____ is a branch of mathematics concerning the study of structure, relation and quantity.
    a. Algebra0
    b. Concept
    c. Undefined
    d. Undefined

62. In mathematics, a _____ is the result of multiplying, or an expression that identifies factors to be multiplied.
    a. Thing
    b. Product0
    c. Undefined
    d. Undefined

63. In mathematics, the _____ inverse of a number x, denoted 1/x or x^{-1}, is the number which, when multiplied by x, yields 1. The _____ inverse of x is also called the reciprocal of x.
    a. Multiplicative0
    b. Thing
    c. Undefined
    d. Undefined

64. In mathematics, a _____ is the end result of a division problem. It can also be expressed as the number of times the divisor divides into the dividend.
    a. Thing
    b. Quotient0
    c. Undefined
    d. Undefined

65. Recurring or _____ are numbers which when expressed as decimals have a set of "final" digits which repeat an infinite number of times.
    a. Thing
    b. Repeating decimals0
    c. Undefined
    d. Undefined

66. In mathematics, factorization (British English: factorisation) or factoring is the decomposition of an object (for example, a number, a polynomial, or a matrix) into a product of other objects, or _____, which when multiplied together give the original.
    a. Factors0
    b. Thing
    c. Undefined
    d. Undefined

67. _____ is a payment made by a company to its shareholders
    a. Dividend0
    b. Thing
    c. Undefined
    d. Undefined

Chapter 1. Review of Real Numbers

68. A _____ is the result of the addition of a set of numbers. The numbers may be natural numbers, complex numbers, matrices, or still more complicated objects. An infinite _____ is a subtle procedure known as a series.
   a. Sum0
   b. Thing
   c. Undefined
   d. Undefined

69. Equivalence is the condition of being _____ or essentially equal.
   a. Thing
   b. Equivalent0
   c. Undefined
   d. Undefined

70. The _____ of two integers is the smallest positive integer that is a multiple of both intergers.
   a. Thing
   b. Least common multiple0
   c. Undefined
   d. Undefined

71. In mathematics, the _____ divisor of two non-zero integers, is the largest positive integer that divides both numbers without remainder.
   a. Greatest common0
   b. Thing
   c. Undefined
   d. Undefined

72. In Math the greates common divisor sometimes known as the _____ of two non- zero integers.
   a. Greatest common factor0
   b. Thing
   c. Undefined
   d. Undefined

73. _____ is the largest positive integer that divides both numbers without remainder.
   a. Common Factor0
   b. Thing
   c. Undefined
   d. Undefined

74. In mathematics, _____ is the decomposition of an object into a product of other objects, or factors, which when multiplied together give the original.
   a. Factoring0
   b. Thing
   c. Undefined
   d. Undefined

75. _____, in number theory is the process of breaking down a composite number into smaller non-trivial divisors, which when multiplied together equal the original integer.
   a. Integer factorization0
   b. Thing
   c. Undefined
   d. Undefined

76. The _____ of a positive integer are the prime numbers that divide into that integer exactly, without leaving a remainder. The process of finding these numbers is called integer factorization, or prime factorization.
   a. Thing
   b. Prime factor0
   c. Undefined
   d. Undefined

77. _____ are objects, characters, or other concrete representations of ideas, concepts, or other abstractions.
   a. Thing
   b. Symbols0
   c. Undefined
   d. Undefined

78. In mathematics, _____ growth occurs when the growth rate of a function is always proportional to the function's current size.
   a. Thing
   b. Exponential0
   c. Undefined
   d. Undefined

79. _____ has many meanings, most of which simply .
   a. Power0
   b. Thing
   c. Undefined
   d. Undefined

80. _____, either of the curved-bracket punctuation marks that together make a set of _____
   a. Thing
   b. Parentheses0
   c. Undefined
   d. Undefined

81. In arithmetic and algebra, when a number or expression is both preceded and followed by a binary operation, an _____ is required for which operation should be applied first.
   a. Order of operations0
   b. Thing
   c. Undefined
   d. Undefined

82. In abstract algebra, _____ consists of sets with binary operations that satisfy certain axioms.
   a. Grouping0
   b. Thing
   c. Undefined
   d. Undefined

83. The _____ is a property of multiplication or addition where the product or sum remains the same, regardless of whether or not the order of the addends or factors are changed.
   a. Commutative property0
   b. Thing
   c. Undefined
   d. Undefined

84. In mathematics, and in particular in abstract algebra, the _____ is a property of binary operations that generalises the distributive law from elementary algebra.
   a. Thing
   b. Distributive property0
   c. Undefined
   d. Undefined

85. An _____ is a number which is involved in addition. Numbers being added are considered to be the addends.
   a. Thing
   b. Addend0
   c. Undefined
   d. Undefined

86. In mathematics and the mathematical sciences, a _____ is a fixed, but possibly unspecified, value. This is in contrast to a variable, which is not fixed.
   a. Constant0
   b. Thing
   c. Undefined
   d. Undefined

87. _____ is a fixed, but possibly unspecified, value. This is in contrast to a variable, which is not fixed.
   a. Thing
   b. Constant term0
   c. Undefined
   d. Undefined

88. In mathematics, a _____ is a constant multiplicative factor of a certain object. The object can be such things as a variable, a vector, a function, etc. For example, the _____ of $9x^2$ is 9.
   a. Coefficient0
   b. Thing
   c. Undefined
   d. Undefined

89. In mathematics, _____ expressions is used to reduce the expression into the lowest possible term.
   a. Simplifying0
   b. Thing
   c. Undefined
   d. Undefined

90. In classical geometry, a _____ of a circle or sphere is any line segment from its center to its boundary. By extension, the _____ of a circle or sphere is the length of any such segment. The _____ is half the diameter. In science and engineering the term _____ of curvature is commonly used as a synonym for _____.
   a. Radius0
   b. Thing
   c. Undefined
   d. Undefined

91. In mathematics, a _____ is a quadric surface, with the following equation in Cartesian coordinates: $(x/_a)^2 + (y/_b)^2 = 1$.
   a. Cylinder0
   b. Thing
   c. Undefined
   d. Undefined

92. The _____ of a right circular cone is the distance from any point on the circle to the apex of the cone.
   a. Thing
   b. Slant height0
   c. Undefined
   d. Undefined

93. _____ is a three-dimensional geometric shape formed by straight lines through a fixed point vertex to the points of a fixed curve directrix.
   a. Right circular cone0
   b. Thing
   c. Undefined
   d. Undefined

94. A _____ is a three-dimensional geometric shape formed by straight lines through a fixed point (vertex) to the points of a fixed curve (directrix)
   a. Cone0
   b. Concept
   c. Undefined
   d. Undefined

95. In mathematics, defined and _____ are used to explain whether or not expressions have meaningful, sensible, and unambiguous values.
   a. Thing
   b. Undefined0
   c. Undefined
   d. Undefined

96. A _____ is a quantity that denotes the proportional amount or magnitude of one quantity relative to another.
   a. Thing
   b. Ratio0
   c. Undefined
   d. Undefined

97. The plus and _____ signs are mathematical symbols used to represent the notions of positive and negative as well as the operations of addition and subtraction.

Chapter 1. Review of Real Numbers

a. Minus0
b. Thing
c. Undefined
d. Undefined

98. In combinatorial mathematics, a _____ is an un-ordered collection of unique elements.
   a. Concept
   b. Combination0
   c. Undefined
   d. Undefined

99. A _____ is a three-dimensional solid object bounded by six square faces, facets, or sides, with three meeting at each vertex.
   a. Cube0
   b. Thing
   c. Undefined
   d. Undefined

100. In plane geometry, a _____ is a polygon with four equal sides, four right angles, and parallel opposite sides. In algebra, the _____ of a number is that number multiplied by itself.
   a. Square0
   b. Thing
   c. Undefined
   d. Undefined

101. U.S. liquid _____ is legally defined as 231 cubic inches, and is equal to 3.785411784 litres or abotu 0.13368 cubic feet. This is the most common definition of a _____. The U.S. fluid ounce is defined as 1/128 of a U.S. _____.
   a. Gallon0
   b. Thing
   c. Undefined
   d. Undefined

102. _____ is a kind of property which exists as magnitude or multitude. It is among the basic classes of things along with quality, substance, change, and relation.
   a. Thing
   b. Amount0
   c. Undefined
   d. Undefined

103. A _____ is a special kind of ratio, indicating a relationship between two measurements with different units, such as miles to gallons or cents to pounds.
   a. Rate0
   b. Thing
   c. Undefined
   d. Undefined

104. In chemistry, a _____ is substance made by combining two or more different materials in such a way that no chemical reaction occurs.
   a. Thing
   b. Mixture0
   c. Undefined
   d. Undefined

105. The _____ is that number multiplied by itself.
   a. Square of a number0
   b. Thing
   c. Undefined
   d. Undefined

106. In sociology and biology a _____ is the collection of people or organisms of a particular species living in a given geographic area or space, usually measured by a census.

Chapter 1. Review of Real Numbers

a. Population0
b. Thing
c. Undefined
d. Undefined

107. _____ or investing is a term with several closely-related meanings in business management, finance and economics, related to saving or deferring consumption.
   a. Thing
   b. Investment0
   c. Undefined
   d. Undefined

108. _____ is the transport of people on a trip/journey or the process or time involved in a person or object moving from one location to another.
   a. Travel0
   b. Thing
   c. Undefined
   d. Undefined

109. A _____ is one of the basic shapes of geometry: a polygon with three vertices and three sides which are straight line segments.
   a. Thing
   b. Triangle0
   c. Undefined
   d. Undefined

110. _____, Greek for "knowledge of nature," is the branch of science concerned with the discovery and characterization of universal laws which govern matter, energy, space, and time.
   a. Thing
   b. Physics0
   c. Undefined
   d. Undefined

111. _____ is defined as the rate of change or derivative with respect to time of velocity.
   a. Thing
   b. Acceleration0
   c. Undefined
   d. Undefined

112. _____ is the property of a physical object that quantifies the amount of matter and energy it is equivalent to.
   a. Mass0
   b. Thing
   c. Undefined
   d. Undefined

113. In mathematics, a _____ of a number x is a number r such that $r^2 = x$, or in words, a number r whose square (the result of multiplying the number by itself) is x.
   a. Square root0
   b. Thing
   c. Undefined
   d. Undefined

114. In mathematics, a _____ of a complex-valued function f is a member x of the domain of f such that f(x) vanishes at x, that is, x : f (x) = 0.
   a. Thing
   b. Root0
   c. Undefined
   d. Undefined

115. _____ forms part of thinking. Considered the most complex of all intellectual functions, _____ has been defined as higher-order cognitive process that requires the modulation and control of more routine or fundamental skills.
   a. Problem solving0
   b. Thing
   c. Undefined
   d. Undefined

Chapter 1. Review of Real Numbers 13

116. _____ was a Hungarian mathematician.
 a. Person
 b. George Polya0
 c. Undefined
 d. Undefined

117. Initial objects are also called _____, and terminal objects are also called final.
 a. Thing
 b. Coterminal0
 c. Undefined
 d. Undefined

118. A _____ is a negotiable instrument instructing a financial institution to pay a specific amount of a specific currency from a specific demand account held in the maker/depositor's name with that institution. Both the maker and payee may be natural persons or legal entities.
 a. Check0
 b. Thing
 c. Undefined
 d. Undefined

119. The _____ of a solid object is the three-dimensional concept of how much space it occupies, often quantified numerically.
 a. Volume0
 b. Thing
 c. Undefined
 d. Undefined

120. _____ is a concept in traditional logic referring to a "type of immediate inference in which from a given proposition another proposition is inferred which has as its subject the predicate of the original proposition and as its predicate the subject of the original proposition (the quality of the proposition being retained)."
 a. Conversion0
 b. Concept
 c. Undefined
 d. Undefined

121. _____ is the portion of a solid – normally a cone or pyramid – which lies between two parallel planes cutting the solid.
 a. Truncated pyramid0
 b. Thing
 c. Undefined
 d. Undefined

122. A _____ is an individual or household that purchases and uses goods and services generated within the economy.
 a. Thing
 b. Consumer0
 c. Undefined
 d. Undefined

123. In mathematics, a _____ is the set of all points in three-dimensional space (R^3) which are at distance r from a fixed point of that space, where r is a positive real number called the radius of the _____. The fixed point is called the center or centre, and is not part of the _____ itself.
 a. Thing
 b. Sphere0
 c. Undefined
 d. Undefined

124. _____ is mass m per unit volume V.
 a. Density0
 b. Thing
 c. Undefined
 d. Undefined

125. A frame of _____ is a particular perspective from which the universe is observed.

a. Thing
c. Undefined
b. Reference0
d. Undefined

126. In mathematics, _____ is a property that a binary operation can have. Within an expression containing two or more of the same associative operators in a row, the order of operations does not matter as long as the sequence of the operands is not changed.
    a. Thing
    b. Associativity0
    c. Undefined
    d. Undefined

127. The payment of _____ as remuneration for services rendered or products sold is a common way to reward sales people.
    a. Commission0
    b. Thing
    c. Undefined
    d. Undefined

128. _____ is a statistical time-series measure of a weighted average of prices of a specified set of goods and services purchased by consumers
    a. Consumer price index0
    b. Thing
    c. Undefined
    d. Undefined

129. The word _____ is used in a variety of ways in mathematics.
    a. Index0
    b. Thing
    c. Undefined
    d. Undefined

130. _____ is a way of expressing a number as a fraction of 100 per cent meaning "per hundred".
    a. Percent0
    b. Thing
    c. Undefined
    d. Undefined

131. _____ is a physical property of a system that underlies the common notions of hot and cold; something that is hotter has the greater _____.
    a. Thing
    b. Temperature0
    c. Undefined
    d. Undefined

Chapter 2. First-Degree Equations and Inequalities

1. In chemistry, a _____ is substance made by combining two or more different materials in such a way that no chemical reaction occurs.
   a. Thing
   b. Mixture0
   c. Undefined
   d. Undefined

2. In mathematics, _____ is an elementary arithmetic operation. When one of the numbers is a whole number, _____ is the repeated sum of the other number.
   a. Multiplication0
   b. Thing
   c. Undefined
   d. Undefined

3. A _____ is a symbolic representation denoting a quantity or expression. It often represents an "unknown" quantity that has the potential to change.
   a. Thing
   b. Variable0
   c. Undefined
   d. Undefined

4. Two mathematical objects are equal if and only if they are precisely the same in every way. This defines a binary relation, _____, denoted by the sign of _____ "=" in such a way that the statement "x = y" means that x and y are equal.
   a. Thing
   b. Equality0
   c. Undefined
   d. Undefined

5. An _____ is a combination of numbers, operators, grouping symbols and/or free variables and bound variables arranged in a meaningful way which can be evaluated..
   a. Thing
   b. Expression0
   c. Undefined
   d. Undefined

6. In mathematics, a _____ of a complex-valued function f is a member x of the domain of f such that f(x) vanishes at x, that is, x : f (x) = 0.
   a. Root0
   b. Thing
   c. Undefined
   d. Undefined

7. An _____ is an equality that remains true regardless of the values of any variables that appear within it, to distinguish it from an equality which is true under more particular conditions.
   a. Identity0
   b. Thing
   c. Undefined
   d. Undefined

8. In banking and accountancy, the outstanding _____ is the amount of money owned, or due, that remains in a deposit account or a loan account at a given date, after all past remittances, payments and withdrawal have been accounted for.
   a. Thing
   b. Balance0
   c. Undefined
   d. Undefined

9. In mathematics, there are several meanings of _____ depending on the subject.
   a. Degree0
   b. Thing
   c. Undefined
   d. Undefined

Chapter 2. First-Degree Equations and Inequalities

10. The _____, the average in everyday English, which is also called the arithmetic _____ (and is distinguished from the geometric _____ or harmonic _____). The average is also called the sample _____. The expected value of a random variable, which is also called the population _____.
   a. Mean0
   b. Thing
   c. Undefined
   d. Undefined

11. In mathematics and the mathematical sciences, a _____ is a fixed, but possibly unspecified, value. This is in contrast to a variable, which is not fixed.
   a. Constant0
   b. Thing
   c. Undefined
   d. Undefined

12. In mathematics, the additive inverse, or _____ of a number n is the number that, when added to n, yields zero. The additive inverse of n is denoted −n. For example, 7 is −7, because 7 + (−7) = 0, and the additive inverse of −0.3 is 0.3, because −0.3 + 0.3 = 0.
   a. Opposite0
   b. Thing
   c. Undefined
   d. Undefined

13. _____ is a fixed, but possibly unspecified, value. This is in contrast to a variable, which is not fixed.
   a. Thing
   b. Constant term0
   c. Undefined
   d. Undefined

14. In mathematics, the _____ of a number n is the number that, when added to n, yields zero. The _____ of n is denoted −n. For example, 7 is −7, because 7 + (−7) = 0, and the _____ of −0.3 is 0.3, because −0.3 + 0.3 = 0.
   a. Additive inverse0
   b. Thing
   c. Undefined
   d. Undefined

15. In mathematics, _____ expressions is used to reduce the expression into the lowest possible term.
   a. Thing
   b. Simplifying0
   c. Undefined
   d. Undefined

16. A _____ is a negotiable instrument instructing a financial institution to pay a specific amount of a specific currency from a specific demand account held in the maker/depositor's name with that institution. Both the maker and payee may be natural persons or legal entities.
   a. Thing
   b. Check0
   c. Undefined
   d. Undefined

17. Equivalence is the condition of being _____ or essentially equal.
   a. Thing
   b. Equivalent0
   c. Undefined
   d. Undefined

18. In mathematics, the multiplicative inverse of a number x, denoted $1/x$ or x^{-1}, is the number which, when multiplied by x, yields 1. The multiplicative inverse of x is also called the _____ of x.
   a. Thing
   b. Reciprocal0
   c. Undefined
   d. Undefined

Chapter 2. First-Degree Equations and Inequalities

19. In mathematics, a _____ is a constant multiplicative factor of a certain object. The object can be such things as a variable, a vector, a function, etc. For example, the _____ of $9x^2$ is 9.
    a. Thing
    b. Coefficient0
    c. Undefined
    d. Undefined

20. In mathematics, and in particular in abstract algebra, the _____ is a property of binary operations that generalises the distributive law from elementary algebra.
    a. Distributive property0
    b. Thing
    c. Undefined
    d. Undefined

21. A _____ of a number is the product of that number with any integer.
    a. Multiple0
    b. Thing
    c. Undefined
    d. Undefined

22. The _____ of two integers is the smallest positive integer that is a multiple of both intergers.
    a. Thing
    b. Least common multiple0
    c. Undefined
    d. Undefined

23. A _____ is the part of a fraction that tells how many equal parts make up a whole, and which is used in the name of the fraction: "halves", "thirds", "fourths" or "quarters", "fifths" and so on.
    a. Denominator0
    b. Concept
    c. Undefined
    d. Undefined

24. A _____ is a compensation which workers receive in exchange for their labor.
    a. Wage0
    b. Thing
    c. Undefined
    d. Undefined

25. A _____ is the result of the addition of a set of numbers. The numbers may be natural numbers, complex numbers, matrices, or still more complicated objects. An infinite _____ is a subtle procedure known as a series.
    a. Sum0
    b. Thing
    c. Undefined
    d. Undefined

26. _____ are a measure of time.
    a. Thing
    b. Minutes0
    c. Undefined
    d. Undefined

27. _____ is a form of periodic payment from an employer to an employee, which is specified in an employment contract.
    a. Gross pay0
    b. Thing
    c. Undefined
    d. Undefined

28. A _____ is a form of periodic payment from an employer to an employee, which is specified in an employment contract.
    a. Thing
    b. Salary0
    c. Undefined
    d. Undefined

Chapter 2. First-Degree Equations and Inequalities

29. In set theory and other branches of mathematics, the _____ of a collection of sets is the set that contains everything that belongs to any of the sets, but nothing else.
    a. Union0
    b. Thing
    c. Undefined
    d. Undefined

30. In economics _____ means before deductions brutto, e.g. _____ domestic or national product, or _____ profit or income
    a. Gross0
    b. Thing
    c. Undefined
    d. Undefined

31. _____, in law and economics, is a form of risk management primarily used to hedge against the risk of a contingent loss.
    a. Thing
    b. Insurance0
    c. Undefined
    d. Undefined

32. A _____ is an individual or household that purchases and uses goods and services generated within the economy.
    a. Consumer0
    b. Thing
    c. Undefined
    d. Undefined

33. _____ is a synonym for information.
    a. Data0
    b. Thing
    c. Undefined
    d. Undefined

34. _____ is a way of expressing a number as a fraction of 100 per cent meaning "per hundred".
    a. Percent0
    b. Thing
    c. Undefined
    d. Undefined

35. In mathematics, a _____ may be described informally as a number that can be given by an infinite decimal representation.
    a. Thing
    b. Real number0
    c. Undefined
    d. Undefined

36. _____ are characters from a logographic or partly logographic writing system. The term originally referred to the Eygptian heiroglphics, but is also applied to the ancient Cretan Luwian, Mayan and Mi'kmaq scripts, and occassionally also to Chinese characters.
    a. Hieroglyphics0
    b. Thing
    c. Undefined
    d. Undefined

37. The _____ , is named after Alexander Henry Rhind, a Scottish antiquarian, who purchased the papyrus in 1858 in Luxor, Egypt; it was apparently found during illegal excavations in or near the Ramesseum.
    a. Thing
    b. Rhind papyrus0
    c. Undefined
    d. Undefined

Chapter 2. First-Degree Equations and Inequalities

38. The _____ are the only integral domain whose positive elements are well-ordered, and in which order is preserved by addition. Like the natural numbers, the _____ form a countably infinite set. The set of all _____ is usually denoted in mathematics by a boldface Z .
   a. Integers0
   b. Thing
   c. Undefined
   d. Undefined

39. _____ means in succession or back-to-back
   a. Thing
   b. Consecutive0
   c. Undefined
   d. Undefined

40. In mathematics, a _____ of an integer n, also called a factor of n, is an integer which evenly divides n without leaving a remainder.
   a. Thing
   b. Divisor0
   c. Undefined
   d. Undefined

41. In mathematics, a _____ is the result of multiplying, or an expression that identifies factors to be multiplied.
   a. Thing
   b. Product0
   c. Undefined
   d. Undefined

42. In common philosophical language, a proposition or _____, is the content of an assertion, that is, it is true-or-false and defined by the meaning of a particular piece of language.
   a. Concept
   b. Statement0
   c. Undefined
   d. Undefined

43. The _____ of measurement are a globally standardized and modernized form of the metric system.
   a. Units0
   b. Thing
   c. Undefined
   d. Undefined

44. The plus and _____ signs are mathematical symbols used to represent the notions of positive and negative as well as the operations of addition and subtraction.
   a. Minus0
   b. Thing
   c. Undefined
   d. Undefined

45. _____ is a kind of property which exists as magnitude or multitude. It is among the basic classes of things along with quality, substance, change, and relation.
   a. Amount0
   b. Thing
   c. Undefined
   d. Undefined

46. _____ is the transport of people on a trip/journey or the process or time involved in a person or object moving from one location to another.
   a. Travel0
   b. Thing
   c. Undefined
   d. Undefined

47. A _____ is a special kind of ratio, indicating a relationship between two measurements with different units, such as miles to gallons or cents to pounds.

a. Thing
b. Rate0
c. Undefined
d. Undefined

48. In botany, _____ are above-ground plant organs specialized for photosynthesis. Their characteristics are typically analyzed by using Fiobonacci's sequences.
    a. Leaves0
    b. Thing
    c. Undefined
    d. Undefined

49. In mathematics, an _____, mean, or central tendency of a data set refers to a measure of the "middle" or "expected" value of the data set.
    a. Concept
    b. Average0
    c. Undefined
    d. Undefined

50. In mathematics, a _____ is a two-dimensional manifold or surface that is perfectly flat.
    a. Thing
    b. Plane0
    c. Undefined
    d. Undefined

51. In mathematics, _____ are two-dimensional manifolds or surfaces that are perfectly flat.
    a. Planes0
    b. Thing
    c. Undefined
    d. Undefined

52. U.S. liquid _____ is legally defined as 231 cubic inches, and is equal to 3.785411784 litres or abotu 0.13368 cubic feet. This is the most common definition of a _____. The U.S. fluid ounce is defined as 1/128 of a U.S. _____.
    a. Thing
    b. Gallon0
    c. Undefined
    d. Undefined

53. Transport or _____ is the movement of people and goods from one place to another.
    a. Transportation0
    b. Thing
    c. Undefined
    d. Undefined

54. _____ is an adjective usually refering to being in the centre.
    a. Thing
    b. Central0
    c. Undefined
    d. Undefined

55. In _____ algebra, a *-ring is an associative ring with an antilinear, antiautomorphism * : A ¨ A which is an involution.
    a. Star0
    b. Thing
    c. Undefined
    d. Undefined

56. In physics, an _____ is the path that an object makes around another object while under the influence of a source of centripetal force, such as gravity.
    a. Orbit0
    b. Thing
    c. Undefined
    d. Undefined

Chapter 2. First-Degree Equations and Inequalities

57. A _____, as defined by the International Astronomical Union, is a celestial body orbiting a star or stellar remnant that is massive enough to be rounded by its own gravity, not massive enough to cause thermonuclear fusion in its core, and has cleared its neighboring region of planetesimals.
   a. Planet0
   b. Thing
   c. Undefined
   d. Undefined

58. A _____ is a unit of length, usually used to measure distance, in a number of different systems, including Imperial units, United States customary units and Norwegian/Swedish mil. Its size can vary from system to system, but in each is between 1 and 10 kilometers. In contemporary English contexts _____ refers to either:
   a. Thing
   b. Mile0
   c. Undefined
   d. Undefined

59. _____ is the fee paid on borrowed money.
   a. Interest0
   b. Thing
   c. Undefined
   d. Undefined

60. An _____ is the fee paid on borrow money.
   a. Interest rate0
   b. Concept
   c. Undefined
   d. Undefined

61. _____ or investing is a term with several closely-related meanings in business management, finance and economics, related to saving or deferring consumption.
   a. Thing
   b. Investment0
   c. Undefined
   d. Undefined

62. A _____ or CD is a time deposit, a financial product commonly offered to consumers by banks, thrift institutions, and credit unions.
   a. Thing
   b. Certificate of deposit0
   c. Undefined
   d. Undefined

63. A _____ is the part of the dividend that is left over when the dividend is not evenly divisible by the divisor.
   a. Remainder0
   b. Thing
   c. Undefined
   d. Undefined

64. The _____ (symbol _____) and the millibar (symbol mbar, also mb) are units of pressure.
   a. Bar0
   b. Thing
   c. Undefined
   d. Undefined

65. A _____ is a craftsman who creates jewelry using jewels, precious metals, or other substances.
   a. Thing
   b. Jeweler0
   c. Undefined
   d. Undefined

66. _____ finance, in finance, a debt security, issued by Issuer
   a. Thing
   b. Bond0
   c. Undefined
   d. Undefined

Chapter 2. First-Degree Equations and Inequalities

67. _____ is an expression of the effective interest rate that will be paid on a loan, taking into account one-time fees and standardizing the way the rate is expressed.
   a. Thing
   b. Annual percentage rate0
   c. Undefined
   d. Undefined

68. _____ are payments to distribution channel members for performing some function .
   a. Thing
   b. Trade discounts0
   c. Undefined
   d. Undefined

69. A _____ is the sum of the elements of a sequence.
   a. Series0
   b. Thing
   c. Undefined
   d. Undefined

70. In finance and economics, _____ is the process of finding the present value of an amount of cash at some future date, and along with compounding cash forms the basis of time value of money calculations.
   a. Discount0
   b. Thing
   c. Undefined
   d. Undefined

71. An _____ or member of a set is an object that when collected together make up the set.
   a. Element0
   b. Thing
   c. Undefined
   d. Undefined

72. A _____ is a set of possible values that a variable can take on in order to satisfy a given set of conditions, which may include equations and inequalities.
   a. Thing
   b. Solution set0
   c. Undefined
   d. Undefined

73. In mathematics, an _____ is a statement about the relative size or order of two objects.
   a. Thing
   b. Inequality0
   c. Undefined
   d. Undefined

74. Mathematical _____ is used to represent ideas.
   a. Notation0
   b. Thing
   c. Undefined
   d. Undefined

75. _____ is a mathematical science pertaining to the collection, analysis, interpretation or explanation, and presentation of data. It is applicable to a wide variety of academic disciplines, from the physical and social sciences to the humanities.
   a. Statistics0
   b. Thing
   c. Undefined
   d. Undefined

76. _____ element of an element x with respect to a binary operation * with identity element e is an element y such that $x * y = y * x = e$. In particular,
   a. Inverse0
   b. Thing
   c. Undefined
   d. Undefined

Chapter 2. First-Degree Equations and Inequalities

77. In mathematics, the _____ inverse, or opposite, of a number n is the number that, when added to n, yields zero. The _____ inverse of n is denoted −n.
    a. Thing
    b. Additive0
    c. Undefined
    d. Undefined

78. In elementary algebra, an _____ is a set that contains every real number between two indicated numbers and may contain the two numbers themselves.
    a. Interval0
    b. Thing
    c. Undefined
    d. Undefined

79. _____ is the notation in which permitted values for a variable are expressed as ranging over a certain interval; "5 < x < 9" is an example of the application of _____.
    a. Thing
    b. Interval notation0
    c. Undefined
    d. Undefined

80. A _____ is a number that is less than zero.
    a. Negative number0
    b. Thing
    c. Undefined
    d. Undefined

81. _____, either of the curved-bracket punctuation marks that together make a set of _____
    a. Thing
    b. Parentheses0
    c. Undefined
    d. Undefined

82. _____ interest refers to the fact that whenever interest is calculated, it is based not only on the original principal, but also on any unpaid interest that has been added to the principal.
    a. Thing
    b. Compound0
    c. Undefined
    d. Undefined

83. _____ is a syntactic operation on sentences, or the symbol for such an operation, that corresponds to a logical operation on the logical values of those sentences.
    a. Thing
    b. Connective0
    c. Undefined
    d. Undefined

84. In mathematics, the _____, or members of a set or more generally a class are all those objects which when collected together make up the set or class.
    a. Thing
    b. Elements0
    c. Undefined
    d. Undefined

85. In mathematics, the _____ of two sets A and B is the set that contains all elements of A that also belong to B (or equivalently, all elements of B that also belong to A), but no other elements.
    a. Intersection0
    b. Thing
    c. Undefined
    d. Undefined

86. In mathematics, _____ are essentially word problems that are designed to use mathematical critical thinking in everyday situations.

Chapter 2. First-Degree Equations and Inequalities

    a. Application problems0   b. Thing
    c. Undefined   d. Undefined

87. A _____ is one of the basic shapes of geometry: a polygon with three vertices and three sides which are straight line segments.
    a. Thing   b. Triangle0
    c. Undefined   d. Undefined

88. In mathematics, an inequality is a statement about the relative size or order of two objects. For example 14 > 10, or 14 is _____ 10.
    a. Greater than0   b. Thing
    c. Undefined   d. Undefined

89. In mathematics, a _____ is the end result of a division problem. It can also be expressed as the number of times the divisor divides into the dividend.
    a. Thing   b. Quotient0
    c. Undefined   d. Undefined

90. In geometry, a _____ is defined as a quadrilateral where all four of its angles are right angles.
    a. Thing   b. Rectangle0
    c. Undefined   d. Undefined

91. _____ is the distance around a given two-dimensional object. As a general rule, the _____ of a polygon can always be calculated by adding all the length of the sides together. So, the formula for triangles is P = a + b + c, where a, b and c stand for each side of it. For quadrilaterals the equation is P = a + b + c + d. For equilateral polygons, P = na, where n is the number of sides and a is the side length.
    a. Thing   b. Perimeter0
    c. Undefined   d. Undefined

92. The payment of _____ as remuneration for services rendered or products sold is a common way to reward sales people.
    a. Commission0   b. Thing
    c. Undefined   d. Undefined

93. Acid _____ ratio measures the ability of a company to use its near cash or quick assets to immediately extinguish its current liabilities.
    a. Thing   b. Test0
    c. Undefined   d. Undefined

94. A _____ is a one-dimensional picture in which the integers are shown as specially-marked points evenly spaced on a line.
    a. Thing   b. Number line0
    c. Undefined   d. Undefined

95. In mathematics, the _____ (or modulus) of a real number is its numerical value without regard to its sign.

Chapter 2. First-Degree Equations and Inequalities

a. Absolute value0
b. Thing
c. Undefined
d. Undefined

96. The _____ integers are all the integers from zero on upwards.
   a. Nonnegative0
   b. Thing
   c. Undefined
   d. Undefined

97. _____ is the estimation of a physical quantity such as distance, energy, temperature, or time.
   a. Measurement0
   b. Thing
   c. Undefined
   d. Undefined

98. In mathematics, in the field of group theory, a _____ of a group is a quasisimple subnormal subgroup.
   a. Component0
   b. Concept
   c. Undefined
   d. Undefined

99. In geometry, a _____ (Greek words diairo = divide and metro = measure) of a circle is any straight line segment that passes through the centre and whose endpoints are on the circular boundary, or, in more modern usage, the length of such a line segment. When using the word in the more modern sense, one speaks of the _____ rather than a _____, because all diameters of a circle have the same length. This length is twice the radius. The _____ of a circle is also the longest chord that the circle has.
   a. Thing
   b. Diameter0
   c. Undefined
   d. Undefined

100. _____ has many meanings, most of which simply .
   a. Thing
   b. Power0
   c. Undefined
   d. Undefined

101. In mathematics, an _____ .
   a. Thing
   b. Ellipse0
   c. Undefined
   d. Undefined

102. An _____ is a term used to describe an allocation of money from one person to another.
   a. Thing
   b. Allowance0
   c. Undefined
   d. Undefined

103. _____ is a natural number that has exactly two distinct natural number divisors, which are 1 and the _____ itself.
   a. Thing
   b. Prime number0
   c. Undefined
   d. Undefined

104. In mathematics, a _____ number (or a _____) is a natural number that has exactly two (distinct) natural number divisors, which are 1 and the _____ number itself.
   a. Prime0
   b. Thing
   c. Undefined
   d. Undefined

Chapter 2. First-Degree Equations and Inequalities

105. A _____ is an illustration used in the branch of mathematics known as set theory. It shows all of the possible mathematical or logical relationships between sets.
   a. Thing
   b. Venn diagram0
   c. Undefined
   d. Undefined

106. In Euclidean geometry, a _____ is the set of all points in a plane at a fixed distance, called the radius, from a given point, the center.
   a. Thing
   b. Circle0
   c. Undefined
   d. Undefined

107. A _____ is a set whose members are members of another set or a set contained within another set.
   a. Subset0
   b. Thing
   c. Undefined
   d. Undefined

108. _____ are groups whose members are members of another set or a set contained within another set.
   a. Thing
   b. Subsets0
   c. Undefined
   d. Undefined

109. A _____ is a simplified and structured visual representation of concepts, ideas, constructions, relations, statistical data, anatomy etc used in all aspects of human activities to visualize and clarify the topic.
   a. Thing
   b. Diagram0
   c. Undefined
   d. Undefined

110. A _____ is 360° or 2ð radians.
   a. Turn0
   b. Thing
   c. Undefined
   d. Undefined

111. The _____ of a function is an extension of the concept of a sum, and are identified or found through the use of integration.
   a. Thing
   b. Integral0
   c. Undefined
   d. Undefined

112. _____ is the difference of electrical potential between two points of an electrical or electronic circuit, expressed in volts
   a. Voltage0
   b. Thing
   c. Undefined
   d. Undefined

113. _____ is electromagnetic radiation with a wavelength that is visible to the eye (visible _____) or, in a technical or scientific context, electromagnetic radiation of any wavelength.
   a. Light0
   b. Thing
   c. Undefined
   d. Undefined

114. A _____ is a function that assigns a number to subsets of a given set.
   a. Measure0
   b. Thing
   c. Undefined
   d. Undefined

Chapter 2. First-Degree Equations and Inequalities

115. The _____, in practice often shortened to amp, is a unit of electric current, or amount of electric charge per second.
   a. Thing
   b. Amperes0
   c. Undefined
   d. Undefined

116. The Yakovlev Yak-25, NATO designation _____-A / Mandrake, was a swept wing, turbojet-powered interceptor aircraft and reconnaissance aircraft used by the Soviet Union.
   a. Flashlight0
   b. Thing
   c. Undefined
   d. Undefined

117. _____, in economics and political economy, are the distributions or payments awarded to the various suppliers of the factors of production.
   a. Returns0
   b. Thing
   c. Undefined
   d. Undefined

118. _____ is the production of food, feed, fiber, fuel and other goods by the systematic raizing of plants and animals.
   a. Thing
   b. Agriculture0
   c. Undefined
   d. Undefined

119. The word _____ is used in a variety of ways in mathematics.
   a. Thing
   b. Index0
   c. Undefined
   d. Undefined

120. Compass and straightedge or ruler-and-compass _____ is the _____ of lengths or angles using only an idealized ruler and compass.
   a. Construction0
   b. Thing
   c. Undefined
   d. Undefined

121. _____ is a physical property of a system that underlies the common notions of hot and cold; something that is hotter has the greater _____.
   a. Temperature0
   b. Thing
   c. Undefined
   d. Undefined

122. _____ is a term applied when talking about the movement of air from one place to the next.
   a. Wind speed0
   b. Thing
   c. Undefined
   d. Undefined

123. _____ is a statistical measure of the average length of survival of a living thing.
   a. Life expectancy0
   b. Thing
   c. Undefined
   d. Undefined

124. _____ is the application of tools and a processing medium to the transformation of raw materials into finished goods for sale.
   a. Thing
   b. Manufacturing0
   c. Undefined
   d. Undefined

125. The mathematical concept of a _____ expresses the intuitive idea of deterministic dependence between two quantities, one of which is viewed as primary and the other as secondary. A _____ then is a way to associate a unique output for each input of a specified type, for example, a real number or an element of a given set.
   a. Thing
   b. Function0
   c. Undefined
   d. Undefined

126. In sociology and biology a _____ is the collection of people or organisms of a particular species living in a given geographic area or space, usually measured by a census.
   a. Thing
   b. Population0
   c. Undefined
   d. Undefined

Chapter 3. Linear Functions and Inequalities in Two Variables

1. A _____ is a set of numbers that designate location in a given reference system, such as x,y in a planar _____ system or an x,y,z in a three-dimensional _____ system.
   a. Coordinate0
   b. Thing
   c. Undefined
   d. Undefined

2. In mathematics and its applications, a _____ is a system for assigning an n-tuple of numbers or scalars to each point in an n-dimensional space.
   a. Concept
   b. Coordinate system0
   c. Undefined
   d. Undefined

3. _____ is a branch of mathematics concerning the study of structure, relation and quantity.
   a. Concept
   b. Algebra0
   c. Undefined
   d. Undefined

4. Acid _____ ratio measures the ability of a company to use its near cash or quick assets to immediately extinguish its current liabilities.
   a. Thing
   b. Test0
   c. Undefined
   d. Undefined

5. _____ is the study of geometry using the principles of algebra. _____ can be explained more simply: it is concerned with defining geometrical shapes in a numerical way and extracting numerical information from that representation.
   a. Analytic geometry0
   b. Thing
   c. Undefined
   d. Undefined

6. _____ was a highly influential French philosopher, mathematician, scientist, and writer. Dubbed the "Founder of Modern Philosophy", and the "Father of Modern Mathematics". His theories provided the basis for the calculus of Newton and Leibniz, by applying infinitesimal calculus to the tangent line problem, thus permitting the evolution of that branch of modern mathematics
   a. Person
   b. Descartes0
   c. Undefined
   d. Undefined

7. A _____ is a one-dimensional picture in which the integers are shown as specially-marked points evenly spaced on a line.
   a. Number line0
   b. Thing
   c. Undefined
   d. Undefined

8. In astronomy, geography, geometry and related sciences and contexts, a plane is said to be _____ at a given point if it is locally perpendicular to the gradient of the gravity field, i.e., with the direction of the gravitational force at that point.
   a. Thing
   b. Horizontal0
   c. Undefined
   d. Undefined

9. In mathematics, the _____ of a coordinate system is the point where the axes of the system intersect.
   a. Thing
   b. Origin0
   c. Undefined
   d. Undefined

10. In mathematics, the _____ of two sets A and B is the set that contains all elements of A that also belong to B (or equivalently, all elements of B that also belong to A), but no other elements.
   a. Thing
   b. Intersection0
   c. Undefined
   d. Undefined

11. An _____ is when two lines intersect somewhere on a plane creating a right angle at intersection
   a. Axes0
   b. Thing
   c. Undefined
   d. Undefined

12. A _____ consists of one quarter of the coordinate plane.
   a. Thing
   b. Quadrant0
   c. Undefined
   d. Undefined

13. In mathematics, a _____ is a two-dimensional manifold or surface that is perfectly flat.
   a. Plane0
   b. Thing
   c. Undefined
   d. Undefined

14. An _____ is a collection of two not necessarily distinct objects, one of which is distinguished as the first coordinate and the other as the second coordinate.
   a. Thing
   b. Ordered pair0
   c. Undefined
   d. Undefined

15. _____ is the fee paid on borrowed money.
   a. Thing
   b. Interest0
   c. Undefined
   d. Undefined

16. _____ means of or relating to the French philosopher and mathematician René Descartes.
   a. Thing
   b. Cartesian0
   c. Undefined
   d. Undefined

17. In mathematics, the _____ is used to determine each point uniquely in a plane through two numbers, usually called the x-coordinate and the y-coordinate of the point.
   a. Cartesian coordinate system0
   b. Thing
   c. Undefined
   d. Undefined

18. The _____ is the y- coordinate of a point within a two dimensional coordinate system. It is sometimes used to refer to the axis rather than the distance along the coordinate system.
   a. Ordinate0
   b. Thing
   c. Undefined
   d. Undefined

19. _____ consists of the first element in a coordinate pair. When graphed in the coordinate plane, it is the distance from the y-axis. Frequently called the x coordinate.
   a. Thing
   b. Abscissa0
   c. Undefined
   d. Undefined

20. An _____ is a straight line around which a geometric figure can be rotated.

Chapter 3. Linear Functions and Inequalities in Two Variables

a. Thing
c. Undefined
b. Axis0
d. Undefined

21. In mathematics, a _____ of a complex-valued function f is a member x of the domain of f such that f(x) vanishes at x, that is, x : f (x) = 0.
    a. Thing
    b. Root0
    c. Undefined
    d. Undefined

22. A _____ is a symbolic representation denoting a quantity or expression. It often represents an "unknown" quantity that has the potential to change.
    a. Thing
    b. Variable0
    c. Undefined
    d. Undefined

23. In common philosophical language, a proposition or _____, is the content of an assertion, that is, it is true-or-false and defined by the meaning of a particular piece of language.
    a. Concept
    b. Statement0
    c. Undefined
    d. Undefined

24. _____ is the state of being greater than any finite real or natural number, however large.
    a. Thing
    b. Infinite0
    c. Undefined
    d. Undefined

25. _____ is a relation in Euclidean geometry among the three sides of a right triangle.
    a. Pythagorean Theorem0
    b. Thing
    c. Undefined
    d. Undefined

26. In geometry, a line _____ is a part of a line that is bounded by two end points, and contains every point on the line between its end points.
    a. Concept
    b. Segment0
    c. Undefined
    d. Undefined

27. A _____ is a part of a line that is bounded by two end points, and contains every point on the line between its end points.
    a. Line segment0
    b. Thing
    c. Undefined
    d. Undefined

28. In mathematics, a _____ is a statement that can be proved on the basis of explicitly stated or previously agreed assumptions.
    a. Thing
    b. Theorem0
    c. Undefined
    d. Undefined

29. _____ is the middle point of a line segment.
    a. Midpoint0
    b. Thing
    c. Undefined
    d. Undefined

30. A _____ is one of the basic shapes of geometry: a polygon with three vertices and three sides which are straight line segments.
   a. Triangle0
   b. Thing
   c. Undefined
   d. Undefined

31. In a right triangle, the _____ of the triangle are the two sides that are perpendicular to each other, as opposed to the hypotenuse.
   a. Thing
   b. Legs0
   c. Undefined
   d. Undefined

32. The _____ of a right triangle is the triangle's longest side; the side opposite the right angle.
   a. Hypotenuse0
   b. Thing
   c. Undefined
   d. Undefined

33. _____ has one 90° internal angle a right angle.
   a. Thing
   b. Right triangle0
   c. Undefined
   d. Undefined

34. The _____ integers are all the integers from zero on upwards.
   a. Thing
   b. Nonnegative0
   c. Undefined
   d. Undefined

35. In plane geometry, a _____ is a polygon with four equal sides, four right angles, and parallel opposite sides. In algebra, the _____ of a number is that number multiplied by itself.
   a. Square0
   b. Thing
   c. Undefined
   d. Undefined

36. The _____ is that number multiplied by itself.
   a. Thing
   b. Square of a number0
   c. Undefined
   d. Undefined

37. In mathematics, the _____ (or modulus) of a real number is its numerical value without regard to its sign.
   a. Thing
   b. Absolute value0
   c. Undefined
   d. Undefined

38. In mathematics, a _____ of a number x is a number r such that $r^2 = x$, or in words, a number r whose square (the result of multiplying the number by itself) is x.
   a. Square root0
   b. Thing
   c. Undefined
   d. Undefined

39. In geometry, an _____ is a point at which a line segment or ray terminates.
   a. Endpoint0
   b. Thing
   c. Undefined
   d. Undefined

40. In mathematics, an _____, mean, or central tendency of a data set refers to a measure of the "middle" or "expected" value of the data set.

Chapter 3. Linear Functions and Inequalities in Two Variables

a. Concept
b. Average0
c. Undefined
d. Undefined

41. A _____ is a simplified and structured visual representation of concepts, ideas, constructions, relations, statistical data, anatomy etc used in all aspects of human activities to visualize and clarify the topic.
    a. Thing
    b. Diagram0
    c. Undefined
    d. Undefined

42. _____ is a kind of property which exists as magnitude or multitude. It is among the basic classes of things along with quality, substance, change, and relation.
    a. Amount0
    b. Thing
    c. Undefined
    d. Undefined

43. In mathematics, a _____ is the result of multiplying, or an expression that identifies factors to be multiplied.
    a. Product0
    b. Thing
    c. Undefined
    d. Undefined

44. _____ is a mathematical science pertaining to the collection, analysis, interpretation or explanation, and presentation of data. It is applicable to a wide variety of academic disciplines, from the physical and social sciences to the humanities.
    a. Thing
    b. Statistics0
    c. Undefined
    d. Undefined

45. The _____, the average in everyday English, which is also called the arithmetic _____ (and is distinguished from the geometric _____ or harmonic _____). The average is also called the sample _____. The expected value of a random variable, which is also called the population _____.
    a. Mean0
    b. Thing
    c. Undefined
    d. Undefined

46. _____ is a synonym for information.
    a. Data0
    b. Thing
    c. Undefined
    d. Undefined

47. In mathematics, the conjugate _____ or adjoint matrix of an m-by-n matrix A with complex entries is the n-by-m matrix A* obtained from A by taking the transpose and then taking the complex conjugate of each entry.
    a. Pairs0
    b. Thing
    c. Undefined
    d. Undefined

48. A _____ is a special kind of ratio, indicating a relationship between two measurements with different units, such as miles to gallons or cents to pounds.
    a. Thing
    b. Rate0
    c. Undefined
    d. Undefined

49. In business, particularly accounting, a _____ is the time intervals that the accounts, statement, payments, or other calculations cover.

a. Thing
b. Period0
c. Undefined
d. Undefined

50. In sociology and biology a _____ is the collection of people or organisms of a particular species living in a given geographic area or space, usually measured by a census.
a. Thing
b. Population0
c. Undefined
d. Undefined

51. In mathematics, a _____ may be described informally as a number that can be given by an infinite decimal representation.
a. Real number0
b. Thing
c. Undefined
d. Undefined

52. _____ is a physical property of a system that underlies the common notions of hot and cold; something that is hotter has the greater _____.
a. Thing
b. Temperature0
c. Undefined
d. Undefined

53. _____ is, or relates to, the _____ temperature scale .
a. Thing
b. Celsius0
c. Undefined
d. Undefined

54. In mathematics, there are several meanings of _____ depending on the subject.
a. Thing
b. Degree0
c. Undefined
d. Undefined

55. _____ is a way of expressing a number as a fraction of 100 per cent meaning "per hundred".
a. Percent0
b. Thing
c. Undefined
d. Undefined

56. The payment of _____ as remuneration for services rendered or products sold is a common way to reward sales people.
a. Commission0
b. Thing
c. Undefined
d. Undefined

57. _____ are procedures that allow people to exchange information by one of several methods.
a. Communications0
b. Thing
c. Undefined
d. Undefined

58. _____ element of an element x with respect to a binary operation * with identity element e is an element y such that x * y = y * x = e. In particular,
a. Thing
b. Inverse0
c. Undefined
d. Undefined

59. In mathematics, the _____ inverse, or opposite, of a number n is the number that, when added to n, yields zero. The _____ inverse of n is denoted −n.

Chapter 3. Linear Functions and Inequalities in Two Variables

a. Additive0
b. Thing
c. Undefined
d. Undefined

60. In mathematics, the _____ of a number n is the number that, when added to n, yields zero. The _____ of n is denoted −n. For example, 7 is −7, because 7 + (−7) = 0, and the _____ of −0.3 is 0.3, because −0.3 + 0.3 = 0.
   a. Thing
   b. Additive inverse0
   c. Undefined
   d. Undefined

61. The _____ of measurement are a globally standardized and modernized form of the metric system.
   a. Thing
   b. Units0
   c. Undefined
   d. Undefined

62. The mathematical concept of a _____ expresses the intuitive idea of deterministic dependence between two quantities, one of which is viewed as primary and the other as secondary. A _____ then is a way to associate a unique output for each input of a specified type, for example, a real number or an element of a given set.
   a. Function0
   b. Thing
   c. Undefined
   d. Undefined

63. A _____ is a type of debt. All material things can be lent but this article focuses exclusively on monetary loans. Like all debt instruments, a _____ entails the redistribution of financial assets over time, between the lender and the borrower.
   a. Thing
   b. Loan0
   c. Undefined
   d. Undefined

64. An _____ is the fee paid on borrow money.
   a. Interest rate0
   b. Concept
   c. Undefined
   d. Undefined

65. In Euclidean geometry, a uniform _____ is a linear transformation that enlargers or diminishes objects, and whose _____ factor is the same in all directions. This is also called homothethy.
   a. Scale0
   b. Thing
   c. Undefined
   d. Undefined

66. In mathematics, a _____ of a k-place relation $L \subseteq X_1 \times ... \times X_k$ is one of the sets X_j, $1 \leq j \leq k$. In the special case where k = 2 and $L \subseteq X_1 \times X_2$ is a function $L : X_1 \rightarrow X_2$, it is conventional to refer to X_1 as the _____ of the function and to refer to X_2 as the codomain of the function.
   a. Thing
   b. Domain0
   c. Undefined
   d. Undefined

67. In mathematics, the _____ of a function is the set of all "output" values produced by that function. Given a function $f : A \rightarrow B$, the _____ of f, is defined to be the set $\{x \in B : x = f(a) \text{ for some } a \in A\}$.
   a. Range0
   b. Thing
   c. Undefined
   d. Undefined

68. In mathematics, in the field of group theory, a _____ of a group is a quasisimple subnormal subgroup.

36 *Chapter 3. Linear Functions and Inequalities in Two Variables*

    a. Component0   b. Concept
    c. Undefined   d. Undefined

69. An _____ or member of a set is an object that when collected together make up the set.
    a. Thing   b. Element0
    c. Undefined   d. Undefined

70. In mathematics, the _____ , or members of a set or more generally a class are all those objects which when collected together make up the set or class.
    a. Elements0   b. Thing
    c. Undefined   d. Undefined

71. Mathematical _____ is used to represent ideas.
    a. Thing   b. Notation0
    c. Undefined   d. Undefined

72. In mathematics, the term _____ is applied to certain functions. There are two common ways it is applied: these are related historically, but diverged somewhat during the twentieth century.
    a. Thing   b. Functional0
    c. Undefined   d. Undefined

73. In a function the _____, is the variable which is the value, i.e. the "output", of the function.
    a. Dependent variable0   b. Thing
    c. Undefined   d. Undefined

74. In mathematics, an _____ is any of the arguments, i.e. "inputs", to a function. Thus if we have a function $f(x)$, then x is a _____.
    a. Thing   b. Independent variable0
    c. Undefined   d. Undefined

75. _____ is the design, analysis, and/or construction of works for practical purposes.
    a. Thing   b. Engineering0
    c. Undefined   d. Undefined

76. _____ of an object is its speed in a particular direction.
    a. Velocity0   b. Thing
    c. Undefined   d. Undefined

77. _____ has many meanings, most of which simply .
    a. Power0   b. Thing
    c. Undefined   d. Undefined

78. The metre (or _____, see spelling differences) is a measure of length. It is the basic unit of length in the metric system and in the International System of Units (SI), used around the world for general and scientific purposes.

a. Concept
b. Meter0
c. Undefined
d. Undefined

79. The act of _____ is the calculated approximation of a result which is usable even if input data may be incomplete, uncertain, or noisy.
    a. Estimating0
    b. Thing
    c. Undefined
    d. Undefined

80. _____, Greek for "knowledge of nature," is the branch of science concerned with the discovery and characterization of universal laws which govern matter, energy, space, and time.
    a. Physics0
    b. Thing
    c. Undefined
    d. Undefined

81. _____ is the level of functional and/or metabolic efficiency of an organism at both the micro level.
    a. Health0
    b. Thing
    c. Undefined
    d. Undefined

82. _____ are a measure of time.
    a. Minutes0
    b. Thing
    c. Undefined
    d. Undefined

83. The word _____ comes from the Latin word linearis, which means created by lines.
    a. Thing
    b. Linear0
    c. Undefined
    d. Undefined

84. _____ describes the location of a place on Earth east or west of a north-south line called the Prime Meridian.
    a. Thing
    b. Longitude0
    c. Undefined
    d. Undefined

85. A _____, sea mile or nautimile is a unit of length. It is accepted for use with the International System of Units (SI), but it is not an SI unit.[1] The _____ is used around the world for maritime and aviation purposes. It is commonly used in international law and treaties, especially regarding the limits of territorial waters. It developed from the geographical mile.
    a. Thing
    b. Nautical mile0
    c. Undefined
    d. Undefined

86. A _____ is a unit of length, usually used to measure distance, in a number of different systems, including Imperial units, United States customary units and Norwegian/Swedish mil. Its size can vary from system to system, but in each is between 1 and 10 kilometers. In contemporary English contexts _____ refers to either:
    a. Mile0
    b. Thing
    c. Undefined
    d. Undefined

87. A _____ is a first degree polynomial mathematical function of the form: f(x) = mx + b where m and b are real constants and x is a real variable.
    a. Linear function0
    b. Thing
    c. Undefined
    d. Undefined

88. A _____ is the part of a fraction that tells how many equal parts make up a whole, and which is used in the name of the fraction: "halves", "thirds", "fourths" or "quarters", "fifths" and so on.
   a. Denominator0
   b. Concept
   c. Undefined
   d. Undefined

89. _____ is the symbold used to indicate the nth root of a number
   a. Radical0
   b. Thing
   c. Undefined
   d. Undefined

90. In mathematics, a _____ is a constant multiplicative factor of a certain object. The object can be such things as a variable, a vector, a function, etc. For example, the _____ of $9x^2$ is 9.
   a. Coefficient0
   b. Thing
   c. Undefined
   d. Undefined

91. A _____ of a number is the product of that number with any integer.
   a. Thing
   b. Multiple0
   c. Undefined
   d. Undefined

92. In linear algebra, the _____ of an n-by-n square matrix A is defined to be the sum of the elements on the main diagonal of A,
   a. Trace0
   b. Thing
   c. Undefined
   d. Undefined

93. A _____ is an equation in which each term is either a constant or the product of a constant times the first power of a variable.
   a. Thing
   b. Linear equation0
   c. Undefined
   d. Undefined

94. In mathematics and the mathematical sciences, a _____ is a fixed, but possibly unspecified, value. This is in contrast to a variable, which is not fixed.
   a. Constant0
   b. Thing
   c. Undefined
   d. Undefined

95. _____ is a function whose values do not vary and thus are constant.
   a. Thing
   b. Constant function0
   c. Undefined
   d. Undefined

96. In mathematics, the _____ f is the collection of all ordered pairs . In particular, graph means the graphical representation of this collection, in the form of a curve or surface, together with axes, etc. Graphing on a Cartesian plane is sometimes referred to as curve sketching.
   a. Graph of a function0
   b. Thing
   c. Undefined
   d. Undefined

97. Any point where a graph makes contact with an coordinate axis is called an _____ of the graph

Chapter 3. Linear Functions and Inequalities in Two Variables

   a. Intercept0
   c. Undefined
   b. Thing
   d. Undefined

98. An _____ is a term used to describe an allocation of money from one person to another.
   a. Thing
   b. Allowance0
   c. Undefined
   d. Undefined

99. _____ is a state located in the southern and southwestern regions of the United States of America.
   a. Thing
   b. Texas0
   c. Undefined
   d. Undefined

100. A _____ is a compensation which workers receive in exchange for their labor.
   a. Wage0
   b. Thing
   c. Undefined
   d. Undefined

101. A _____ is a fee added to a customer's bill.
   a. Thing
   b. Service charge0
   c. Undefined
   d. Undefined

102. _____ is a term used in marketing to indicate how much the price of a product is above the cost of producing and distributing the product.
   a. Thing
   b. Markup0
   c. Undefined
   d. Undefined

103. _____ is often used to describe the measurement of the steepness, incline, gradient, or grade of a straight line. The _____ is defined as the ratio of the "rise" divided by the "run" between two points on a line, or in other words, the ratio of the altitude change to the horizontal distance between any two points on the line.
   a. Slope0
   b. Thing
   c. Undefined
   d. Undefined

104. _____ are the basic objects of study in graph theory. Informally speaking, a graph is a set of objects called points, nodes, or vertices connected by links called lines or edges.
   a. Thing
   b. Graphs0
   c. Undefined
   d. Undefined

105. A _____ is a function that assigns a number to subsets of a given set.
   a. Measure0
   b. Thing
   c. Undefined
   d. Undefined

106. A _____ is a quantity that denotes the proportional amount or magnitude of one quantity relative to another.
   a. Ratio0
   b. Thing
   c. Undefined
   d. Undefined

107. In mathematics, defined and _____ are used to explain whether or not expressions have meaningful, sensible, and unambiguous values.

Chapter 3. Linear Functions and Inequalities in Two Variables

    a. Undefined0   b. Thing
    c. Undefined   d. Undefined

108. _____ is a mathematical subject that includes the study of limits, derivatives, integrals, and power series and constitutes a major part of modern university curriculum.
    a. Calculus0   b. Thing
    c. Undefined   d. Undefined

109. In mathematics, a _____ is a countable collection of open covers of a topological space that satisfies certain separation axioms.
    a. Development0   b. Thing
    c. Undefined   d. Undefined

110. In geometry, an _____ of a triangle is a straight line through a vertex and perpendicular to (i.e. forming a right angle with) the opposite side or an extension of the opposite side.
    a. Concept   b. Altitude0
    c. Undefined   d. Undefined

111. A _____ is a unit of length in the metric system, equal to one thousand metres, the current SI base unit of length
    a. Kilometer0   b. Thing
    c. Undefined   d. Undefined

112. _____ are activities that are governed by a set of rules or customs and often engaged in competitively.
    a. Thing   b. Sports0
    c. Undefined   d. Undefined

113. In geometry, a _____ (Greek words diairo = divide and metro = measure) of a circle is any straight line segment that passes through the centre and whose endpoints are on the circular boundary, or, in more modern usage, the length of such a line segment. When using the word in the more modern sense, one speaks of the _____ rather than a _____, because all diameters of a circle have the same length. This length is twice the radius. The _____ of a circle is also the longest chord that the circle has.
    a. Diameter0   b. Thing
    c. Undefined   d. Undefined

114. In elementary algebra, an _____ is a set that contains every real number between two indicated numbers and may contain the two numbers themselves.
    a. Interval0   b. Thing
    c. Undefined   d. Undefined

115. In mathematics, _____ are essentially word problems that are designed to use mathematical critical thinking in everyday situations.
    a. Application problems0   b. Thing
    c. Undefined   d. Undefined

116. _____ is a temperature scale named after the German physicist Daniel Gabriel _____ , who proposed it in 1724.

Chapter 3. Linear Functions and Inequalities in Two Variables 41

 a. Fahrenheit0   b. Thing
 c. Undefined   d. Undefined

117. U.S. liquid _____ is legally defined as 231 cubic inches, and is equal to 3.785411784 litres or abotu 0.13368 cubic feet. This is the most common definition of a _____. The U.S. fluid ounce is defined as 1/128 of a U.S. _____.
 a. Thing   b. Gallon0
 c. Undefined   d. Undefined

118. _____ is the transport of people on a trip/journey or the process or time involved in a person or object moving from one location to another.
 a. Thing   b. Travel0
 c. Undefined   d. Undefined

119. In mathematics, factorization (British English: factorisation) or factoring is the decomposition of an object (for example, a number, a polynomial, or a matrix) into a product of other objects, or _____, which when multiplied together give the original.
 a. Factors0   b. Thing
 c. Undefined   d. Undefined

120. The existence and properties of _____ are the basis of Euclid's parallel postulate. _____ are two lines on the same plane that do not intersect even assuming that lines extend to infinity in either direction.
 a. Parallel lines0   b. Thing
 c. Undefined   d. Undefined

121. In geometry, two lines or planes if one falls on the other in such a way as to create congruent adjacent angles. The term may be used as a noun or adjective. Thus, referring to Figure 1, the line AB is the _____ to CD through the point B.
 a. Perpendicular0   b. Thing
 c. Undefined   d. Undefined

122. In geometry and trigonometry, a _____ is defined as an angle between two straight intersecting lines of ninety degrees, or one-quarter of a circle.
 a. Right angle0   b. Thing
 c. Undefined   d. Undefined

123. In mathematics, the multiplicative inverse of a number x, denoted 1/x or x^{-1}, is the number which, when multiplied by x, yields 1. The multiplicative inverse of x is also called the _____ of x.
 a. Thing   b. Reciprocal0
 c. Undefined   d. Undefined

124. A _____ is a negotiable instrument instructing a financial institution to pay a specific amount of a specific currency from a specific demand account held in the maker/depositor's name with that institution. Both the maker and payee may be natural persons or legal entities.
 a. Thing   b. Check0
 c. Undefined   d. Undefined

Chapter 3. Linear Functions and Inequalities in Two Variables

125. In Euclidean geometry, a _____ is the set of all points in a plane at a fixed distance, called the radius, from a given point, the center.
   a. Thing
   b. Circle0
   c. Undefined
   d. Undefined

126. Initial objects are also called _____, and terminal objects are also called final.
   a. Thing
   b. Coterminal0
   c. Undefined
   d. Undefined

127. In classical geometry, a _____ of a circle or sphere is any line segment from its center to its boundary. By extension, the _____ of a circle or sphere is the length of any such segment. The _____ is half the diameter. In science and engineering the term _____ of curvature is commonly used as a synonym for _____.
   a. Radius0
   b. Thing
   c. Undefined
   d. Undefined

128. In geometry, the _____ of an object is a point in some sense in the middle of the object.
   a. Thing
   b. Center0
   c. Undefined
   d. Undefined

129. In trigonometry, the _____ is a function defined as tan x = $^{\sin x}/_{\cos x}$. The function is so-named because it can be defined as the length of a certain segment of a _____ (in the geometric sense) to the unit circle. In plane geometry, a line is _____ to a curve, at some point, if both line and curve pass through the point with the same direction.
   a. Tangent0
   b. Thing
   c. Undefined
   d. Undefined

130. _____ has two distinct but etymologically-related meanings: one in geometry and one in trigonometry.
   a. Tangent line0
   b. Thing
   c. Undefined
   d. Undefined

131. A _____ is a set of possible values that a variable can take on in order to satisfy a given set of conditions, which may include equations and inequalities.
   a. Thing
   b. Solution set0
   c. Undefined
   d. Undefined

132. In mathematics, an _____ is a statement about the relative size or order of two objects.
   a. Thing
   b. Inequality0
   c. Undefined
   d. Undefined

133. Two mathematical objects are equal if and only if they are precisely the same in every way. This defines a binary relation, _____, denoted by the sign of _____ "=" in such a way that the statement "x = y" means that x and y are equal.
   a. Equality0
   b. Thing
   c. Undefined
   d. Undefined

134. In mathematics, _____ geometry was the traditional name for the geometry of three-dimensional Euclidean space — for practical purposes the kind of space we live in.

a. Solid0   b. Thing
c. Undefined   d. Undefined

135. _____ is a mathematical operation, written a^n, involving two numbers, the base a and the exponent n.
a. Exponentiating0   b. Thing
c. Undefined   d. Undefined

136. _____ is a mathematical operation, written a^n, involving two numbers, the base a and the exponent n.
a. Thing   b. Exponentiation0
c. Undefined   d. Undefined

137. _____ forms part of thinking. Considered the most complex of all intellectual functions, _____ has been defined as higher-order cognitive process that requires the modulation and control of more routine or fundamental skills.
a. Problem solving0   b. Thing
c. Undefined   d. Undefined

138. Johann _____ was a German mathematician and scientist of profound genius who contributed significantly to many fields, including number theory, analysis, differential geometry, geodesy, magnetism, astronomy, and optics. He completed Disquisitiones Arithmeticae, his magnum opus, at the age of twenty-one.
a. Person   b. Carl Friedrich Gauss0
c. Undefined   d. Undefined

139. A _____ is the result of the addition of a set of numbers. The numbers may be natural numbers, complex numbers, matrices, or still more complicated objects. An infinite _____ is a subtle procedure known as a series.
a. Sum0   b. Thing
c. Undefined   d. Undefined

140. In finance, a _____ is collateral that the holder of a position in securities, options, or futures contracts has to deposit to cover the credit risk of his counterparty.
a. Thing   b. Margin0
c. Undefined   d. Undefined

141. In mathematics, a _____ is a mathematical statement which appears likely to be true, but has not been formally proven to be true under the rules of mathematical logic.
a. Conjecture0   b. Concept
c. Undefined   d. Undefined

142. _____ is the notation in which permitted values for a variable are expressed as ranging over a certain interval; "5 < x < 9" is an example of the application of _____.
a. Thing   b. Interval notation0
c. Undefined   d. Undefined

143. _____ is a term applied when talking about the movement of air from one place to the next.
a. Wind speed0   b. Thing
c. Undefined   d. Undefined

144. In combinatorial mathematics, a _____ is an un-ordered collection of unique elements.
   a. Concept
   b. Combination0
   c. Undefined
   d. Undefined

145. The word _____ is used in a variety of ways in mathematics.
   a. Index0
   b. Thing
   c. Undefined
   d. Undefined

146. _____ is a set, with some particular properties and usually some additional structure, such as the operations of addition or multiplication, for instance.
   a. Space0
   b. Thing
   c. Undefined
   d. Undefined

147. A _____ is an individual or household that purchases and uses goods and services generated within the economy.
   a. Consumer0
   b. Thing
   c. Undefined
   d. Undefined

148. In mathematics, _____ are two-dimensional manifolds or surfaces that are perfectly flat.
   a. Planes0
   b. Thing
   c. Undefined
   d. Undefined

149. Compass and straightedge or ruler-and-compass _____ is the _____ of lengths or angles using only an idealized ruler and compass.
   a. Construction0
   b. Thing
   c. Undefined
   d. Undefined

150. _____ or investing is a term with several closely-related meanings in business management, finance and economics, related to saving or deferring consumption.
   a. Thing
   b. Investment0
   c. Undefined
   d. Undefined

151. _____ is the application of tools and a processing medium to the transformation of raw materials into finished goods for sale.
   a. Manufacturing0
   b. Thing
   c. Undefined
   d. Undefined

152. In chemistry, a _____ is substance made by combining two or more different materials in such a way that no chemical reaction occurs.
   a. Mixture0
   b. Thing
   c. Undefined
   d. Undefined

153. _____ is the technique and science of accurately determining the terrestrial or three-dimensional space position of points and the distances and angles between them.

a. Thing
b. Surveying0
c. Undefined
d. Undefined

Chapter 4. Systems of Equations and Inequalities

1. The _____ is used to discard one of the variables in an equation, only to replace it with the actual value when solving multiple equations.
   a. Substitution method0
   b. Thing
   c. Undefined
   d. Undefined

2. The word _____ comes from the Latin word linearis, which means created by lines.
   a. Linear0
   b. Thing
   c. Undefined
   d. Undefined

3. A _____ is an equation in which each term is either a constant or the product of a constant times the first power of a variable.
   a. Linear equation0
   b. Thing
   c. Undefined
   d. Undefined

4. A _____ is a symbolic representation denoting a quantity or expression. It often represents an "unknown" quantity that has the potential to change.
   a. Variable0
   b. Thing
   c. Undefined
   d. Undefined

5. An _____ is a collection of two not necessarily distinct objects, one of which is distinguished as the first coordinate and the other as the second coordinate.
   a. Ordered pair0
   b. Thing
   c. Undefined
   d. Undefined

6. A _____ is a set of numbers that designate location in a given reference system, such as x,y in a planar _____ system or an x,y,z in a three-dimensional _____ system.
   a. Coordinate0
   b. Thing
   c. Undefined
   d. Undefined

7. An _____ is when two lines intersect somewhere on a plane creating a right angle at intersection
   a. Thing
   b. Axes0
   c. Undefined
   d. Undefined

8. A _____ is a negotiable instrument instructing a financial institution to pay a specific amount of a specific currency from a specific demand account held in the maker/depositor's name with that institution. Both the maker and payee may be natural persons or legal entities.
   a. Check0
   b. Thing
   c. Undefined
   d. Undefined

9. _____ are the basic objects of study in graph theory. Informally speaking, a graph is a set of objects called points, nodes, or vertices connected by links called lines or edges.
   a. Thing
   b. Graphs0
   c. Undefined
   d. Undefined

10. _____ is the state of being greater than any finite real or natural number, however large.

Chapter 4. Systems of Equations and Inequalities

    a. Infinite0
    b. Thing
    c. Undefined
    d. Undefined

11. In mathematics, the conjugate _____ or adjoint matrix of an m-by-n matrix A with complex entries is the n-by-m matrix A* obtained from A by taking the transpose and then taking the complex conjugate of each entry.
    a. Pairs0
    b. Thing
    c. Undefined
    d. Undefined

12. In mathematics, the _____ of two sets A and B is the set that contains all elements of A that also belong to B (or equivalently, all elements of B that also belong to A), but no other elements.
    a. Thing
    b. Intersection0
    c. Undefined
    d. Undefined

13. _____ are a set of equations containing multiple variables.
    a. Systems of equations0
    b. Thing
    c. Undefined
    d. Undefined

14. _____ is often used to describe the measurement of the steepness, incline, gradient, or grade of a straight line. The _____ is defined as the ratio of the "rise" divided by the "run" between two points on a line, or in other words, the ratio of the altitude change to the horizontal distance between any two points on the line.
    a. Thing
    b. Slope0
    c. Undefined
    d. Undefined

15. A _____ is the result of the addition of a set of numbers. The numbers may be natural numbers, complex numbers, matrices, or still more complicated objects. An infinite _____ is a subtle procedure known as a series.
    a. Thing
    b. Sum0
    c. Undefined
    d. Undefined

16. _____ is a synonym for information.
    a. Thing
    b. Data0
    c. Undefined
    d. Undefined

17. In sociology and biology a _____ is the collection of people or organisms of a particular species living in a given geographic area or space, usually measured by a census.
    a. Population0
    b. Thing
    c. Undefined
    d. Undefined

18. Two mathematical objects are equal if and only if they are precisely the same in every way. This defines a binary relation, _____, denoted by the sign of _____ "=" in such a way that the statement "x = y" means that x and y are equal.
    a. Equality0
    b. Thing
    c. Undefined
    d. Undefined

19. An _____ is a combination of numbers, operators, grouping symbols and/or free variables and bound variables arranged in a meaningful way which can be evaluated..

Chapter 4. Systems of Equations and Inequalities

   a. Expression0
   c. Undefined
   b. Thing
   d. Undefined

20. In mathematics, in the field of group theory, a _____ of a group is a quasisimple subnormal subgroup.
   a. Component0
   c. Undefined
   b. Concept
   d. Undefined

21. _____ element of an element x with respect to a binary operation * with identity element e is an element y such that $x * y = y * x = e$. In particular,
   a. Thing
   c. Undefined
   b. Inverse0
   d. Undefined

22. In mathematics, the _____ inverse, or opposite, of a number n is the number that, when added to n, yields zero. The _____ inverse of n is denoted −n.
   a. Thing
   c. Undefined
   b. Additive0
   d. Undefined

23. In mathematics, the _____ of a number n is the number that, when added to n, yields zero. The _____ of n is denoted −n. For example, 7 is −7, because $7 + (-7) = 0$, and the _____ of −0.3 is 0.3, because $-0.3 + 0.3 = 0$.
   a. Thing
   c. Undefined
   b. Additive inverse0
   d. Undefined

24. In mathematics, a _____ is a constant multiplicative factor of a certain object. The object can be such things as a variable, a vector, a function, etc. For example, the _____ of $9x^2$ is 9.
   a. Thing
   c. Undefined
   b. Coefficient0
   d. Undefined

25. In mathematics and the mathematical sciences, a _____ is a fixed, but possibly unspecified, value. This is in contrast to a variable, which is not fixed.
   a. Thing
   c. Undefined
   b. Constant0
   d. Undefined

26. Mathematical _____ is used to represent ideas.
   a. Notation0
   c. Undefined
   b. Thing
   d. Undefined

27. A _____ is the part of a fraction that tells how many equal parts make up a whole, and which is used in the name of the fraction: "halves", "thirds", "fourths" or "quarters", "fifths" and so on.
   a. Concept
   c. Undefined
   b. Denominator0
   d. Undefined

28. In Euclidean geometry, an _____ is a closed segment of a differentiable curve in the two-dimensional plane; for example, a circular _____ is a segment of a circle.
   a. Concept
   c. Undefined
   b. Arc0
   d. Undefined

Chapter 4. Systems of Equations and Inequalities

29. In mathematics, a _____ is a two-dimensional manifold or surface that is perfectly flat.
    a. Plane0
    b. Thing
    c. Undefined
    d. Undefined

30. An _____ is a straight line around which a geometric figure can be rotated.
    a. Axis0
    b. Thing
    c. Undefined
    d. Undefined

31. In geometry, two lines or planes if one falls on the other in such a way as to create congruent adjacent angles. The term may be used as a noun or adjective. Thus, referring to Figure 1, the line AB is the _____ to CD through the point B.
    a. Thing
    b. Perpendicular0
    c. Undefined
    d. Undefined

32. In mathematics and its applications, a _____ is a system for assigning an n-tuple of numbers or scalars to each point in an n-dimensional space.
    a. Coordinate system0
    b. Concept
    c. Undefined
    d. Undefined

33. In mathematics, _____ are two-dimensional manifolds or surfaces that are perfectly flat.
    a. Thing
    b. Planes0
    c. Undefined
    d. Undefined

34. In mathematics, a _____ is an n-tuple with n being 3.
    a. Triple0
    b. Thing
    c. Undefined
    d. Undefined

35. _____ is the fee paid on borrowed money.
    a. Interest0
    b. Thing
    c. Undefined
    d. Undefined

36. In computer science an _____ is a data structure that consists of a group of elements having a single name that are accessed by indexing. In most programming languages each element has the same data type and the _____ occupies a continuous area of storage.
    a. Array0
    b. Thing
    c. Undefined
    d. Undefined

37. In mathematics, a _____ is a rectangular table of numbers or, more generally, a table consisting of abstract quantities that can be added and multiplied.
    a. Matrix0
    b. Thing
    c. Undefined
    d. Undefined

38. In algebra, a _____ is a function depending on n that associates a scalar, $\det(A)$, to every $n \times n$ square matrix A.
    a. Determinant0
    b. Thing
    c. Undefined
    d. Undefined

39. An _____ or member of a set is an object that when collected together make up the set.

Chapter 4. Systems of Equations and Inequalities

    a. Element0
    b. Thing
    c. Undefined
    d. Undefined

40. In mathematics, a matrix can be thought of as each row or _____ being a vector. Hence, a space formed by row vectors or _____ vectors are said to be a row space or a _____ space.
    a. Column0
    b. Concept
    c. Undefined
    d. Undefined

41. In plane geometry, a _____ is a polygon with four equal sides, four right angles, and parallel opposite sides. In algebra, the _____ of a number is that number multiplied by itself.
    a. Square0
    b. Thing
    c. Undefined
    d. Undefined

42. _____, verti-bar, vertical line, divider line, or pipe is the name of the character .
    a. Vertical bar0
    b. Thing
    c. Undefined
    d. Undefined

43. The _____ (symbol _____) and the millibar (symbol mbar, also mb) are units of pressure.
    a. Bar0
    b. Thing
    c. Undefined
    d. Undefined

44. In linear algebra, a _____ of a matrix A is the determinant of some smaller square matrix, cut down from A.
    a. Minor0
    b. Thing
    c. Undefined
    d. Undefined

45. In linear algebra, a _____ or minor of a matrix A is the determinant of some smaller square matrix, cut down from A.
    a. Cofactor0
    b. Thing
    c. Undefined
    d. Undefined

46. In common philosophical language, a proposition or _____, is the content of an assertion, that is, it is true-or-false and defined by the meaning of a particular piece of language.
    a. Statement0
    b. Concept
    c. Undefined
    d. Undefined

47. A _____ is a numeral used to indicate a count. The most common use of the word today is to name the part of a fraction that tells the number or count of equal parts.
    a. Thing
    b. Numerator0
    c. Undefined
    d. Undefined

48. _____ (July 31, 1704 - January 4, 1752) was a Swiss mathematician, born in Geneva.
    a. Gabriel Cramer0
    b. Person
    c. Undefined
    d. Undefined

49. In mathematics, defined and _____ are used to explain whether or not expressions have meaningful, sensible, and unambiguous values.

a. Undefined0
b. Thing
c. Undefined
d. Undefined

50. In mathematics, the _____ , or members of a set or more generally a class are all those objects which when collected together make up the set or class.
   a. Thing
   b. Elements0
   c. Undefined
   d. Undefined

51. In linear algebra, the _____ of a square matrix is the diagonal which runs from the top left corner to the bottom right corner.
   a. Main diagonal0
   b. Thing
   c. Undefined
   d. Undefined

52. A _____ can refer to a line joining two nonadjacent vertices of a polygon or polyhedron, or in some contexts any upward or downward sloping line. .
   a. Thing
   b. Diagonal0
   c. Undefined
   d. Undefined

53. In linear algebra, the _____ of a matrix is obtained by combining two matrices in such a way that a matrix of coefficients to which has been added a column of constants corresponds to the right hand side of the equations.
   a. Augmented matrix0
   b. Thing
   c. Undefined
   d. Undefined

54. A _____ of a number is the product of that number with any integer.
   a. Multiple0
   b. Thing
   c. Undefined
   d. Undefined

55. _____ are elementary linear transformations on a matrix which preserve matrix equivalence.
   a. Elementary row operations0
   b. Thing
   c. Undefined
   d. Undefined

56. In mathematics, the multiplicative inverse of a number x, denoted 1/x or x^{-1}, is the number which, when multiplied by x, yields 1. The multiplicative inverse of x is also called the _____ of x.
   a. Thing
   b. Reciprocal0
   c. Undefined
   d. Undefined

57. In mathematics, the additive inverse, or _____ of a number n is the number that, when added to n, yields zero. The additive inverse of n is denoted −n. For example, 7 is −7, because 7 + (−7) = 0, and the additive inverse of −0.3 is 0.3, because −0.3 + 0.3 = 0.
   a. Thing
   b. Opposite0
   c. Undefined
   d. Undefined

58. A _____ is a matrix form used when solving linear systems of equations.
   a. Thing
   b. Row echelon form0
   c. Undefined
   d. Undefined

Chapter 4. Systems of Equations and Inequalities

59. Elementary _____ are simple transformations which can be applied to a matrix without changing the linear system of equations that it represents.
    a. Thing
    b. Row operations0
    c. Undefined
    d. Undefined

60. In mathematics, a matrix is in row _____ if is satisfies the following requirements: • All nonzero rows are above any rows of all zeroes. • The leading coefficient of a row is always strictly to the right of the leading coefficient of the row above it.
    a. Echelon form0
    b. Thing
    c. Undefined
    d. Undefined

61. In mathematics, a _____ is an ordered list of objects. Like a set, it contains members, also called elements or terms, and the number of terms is called the length of the _____. Unlike a set, order matters, and the exact same elements can appear multiple times at different positions in the _____.
    a. Sequence0
    b. Thing
    c. Undefined
    d. Undefined

62. The Gaussian _____ is an algorithm which can be used to determine the solutions of a system of linear equations, to find the rank of a matrix, and to calculate the inverse of an invertible square matrix.
    a. Elimination method0
    b. Thing
    c. Undefined
    d. Undefined

63. _____ is an algorithm which can be used to determine the solutions of a system of linear equations, to find the rank of a matrix, and to calculate the inverse of an invertible square matrix.
    a. Thing
    b. Gaussian elimination0
    c. Undefined
    d. Undefined

64. Johann _____ was a German mathematician and scientist of profound genius who contributed significantly to many fields, including number theory, analysis, differential geometry, geodesy, magnetism, astronomy, and optics. He completed Disquisitiones Arithmeticae, his magnum opus, at the age of twenty-one.
    a. Person
    b. Carl Friedrich Gauss0
    c. Undefined
    d. Undefined

65. In mathematics, _____ is a part of the set theoretic notion of function.
    a. Thing
    b. Image0
    c. Undefined
    d. Undefined

66. In linear algebra, the _____ refers to a matrix consisting of the coefficients of the variables in a set of linear equations.
    a. Coefficient matrix0
    b. Thing
    c. Undefined
    d. Undefined

67. Equivalence is the condition of being _____ or essentially equal.
    a. Thing
    b. Equivalent0
    c. Undefined
    d. Undefined

Chapter 4. Systems of Equations and Inequalities

68. A _____ is a special kind of ratio, indicating a relationship between two measurements with different units, such as miles to gallons or cents to pounds.
   a. Rate0
   b. Thing
   c. Undefined
   d. Undefined

69. In mathematics, _____ are essentially word problems that are designed to use mathematical critical thinking in everyday situations.
   a. Thing
   b. Application problems0
   c. Undefined
   d. Undefined

70. Regrouping is the act of putting ones into groups of 10. For example, the 1 on the far right of 131 would be denoted _____ if the digit of the number being subtracted is larger than 1, such as 131-99.
   a. By 100
   b. Thing
   c. Undefined
   d. Undefined

71. _____ is a kind of property which exists as magnitude or multitude. It is among the basic classes of things along with quality, substance, change, and relation.
   a. Amount0
   b. Thing
   c. Undefined
   d. Undefined

72. _____ is electromagnetic radiation with a wavelength that is visible to the eye (visible _____) or, in a technical or scientific context, electromagnetic radiation of any wavelength.
   a. Light0
   b. Thing
   c. Undefined
   d. Undefined

73. In finance and economics, _____ is the process of finding the present value of an amount of cash at some future date, and along with compounding cash forms the basis of time value of money calculations.
   a. Thing
   b. Discount0
   c. Undefined
   d. Undefined

74. _____ is the transport of people on a trip/journey or the process or time involved in a person or object moving from one location to another.
   a. Thing
   b. Travel0
   c. Undefined
   d. Undefined

75. Compass and straightedge or ruler-and-compass _____ is the _____ of lengths or angles using only an idealized ruler and compass.
   a. Construction0
   b. Thing
   c. Undefined
   d. Undefined

76. In chemistry, a _____ is substance made by combining two or more different materials in such a way that no chemical reaction occurs.
   a. Thing
   b. Mixture0
   c. Undefined
   d. Undefined

77. The _____ of measurement are a globally standardized and modernized form of the metric system.

Chapter 4. Systems of Equations and Inequalities

a. Units0
b. Thing
c. Undefined
d. Undefined

78. A _____ is a landform that extends above the surrounding terrain in a limited area. A _____ is generally steeper than a hill, but there is no universally accepted standard definition for the height of a _____ or a hill although a _____ usually has an identifiable summit.

a. Thing
b. Mountain0
c. Undefined
d. Undefined

79. _____ is the application of tools and a processing medium to the transformation of raw materials into finished goods for sale.

a. Thing
b. Manufacturing0
c. Undefined
d. Undefined

80. _____ or investing is a term with several closely-related meanings in business management, finance and economics, related to saving or deferring consumption.

a. Investment0
b. Thing
c. Undefined
d. Undefined

81. A _____ is the part of the dividend that is left over when the dividend is not evenly divisible by the divisor.

a. Remainder0
b. Thing
c. Undefined
d. Undefined

82. _____ is a mathematical science pertaining to the collection, analysis, interpretation or explanation, and presentation of data. It is applicable to a wide variety of academic disciplines, from the physical and social sciences to the humanities.

a. Thing
b. Statistics0
c. Undefined
d. Undefined

83. A pair of angles are _____ if the sum of their angles is 90°.

a. Complementary0
b. Concept
c. Undefined
d. Undefined

84. A _____ is a function that assigns a number to subsets of a given set.

a. Thing
b. Measure0
c. Undefined
d. Undefined

85. _____ is the level of functional and/or metabolic efficiency of an organism at both the micro level.

a. Thing
b. Health0
c. Undefined
d. Undefined

86. In mathematics, a _____ is a countable collection of open covers of a topological space that satisfies certain separation axioms.

a. Thing
b. Development0
c. Undefined
d. Undefined

Chapter 4. Systems of Equations and Inequalities

87. A _____ is a set of possible values that a variable can take on in order to satisfy a given set of conditions, which may include equations and inequalities.
   a. Solution set0
   b. Thing
   c. Undefined
   d. Undefined

88. In mathematics, an _____ is a statement about the relative size or order of two objects.
   a. Inequality0
   b. Thing
   c. Undefined
   d. Undefined

89. In mathematics, _____ geometry was the traditional name for the geometry of three-dimensional Euclidean space — for practical purposes the kind of space we live in.
   a. Thing
   b. Solid0
   c. Undefined
   d. Undefined

90. In mathematics and more specifically set theory, the _____ set is the unique set which contains no elements.
   a. Empty0
   b. Thing
   c. Undefined
   d. Undefined

91. In set theory, an _____ is a set that is not a finite set. Infinite sets may be countable or uncountable.
   a. Infinite set0
   b. Thing
   c. Undefined
   d. Undefined

92. A _____ is a simplified and structured visual representation of concepts, ideas, constructions, relations, statistical data, anatomy etc used in all aspects of human activities to visualize and clarify the topic.
   a. Diagram0
   b. Thing
   c. Undefined
   d. Undefined

93. Deductive _____ is the kind of _____ in which the conclusion is necessitated by, or reached from, previously known facts (the premises).
   a. Thing
   b. Reasoning0
   c. Undefined
   d. Undefined

94. In linear algebra, the _____ of an n-by-n square matrix A is defined to be the sum of the elements on the main diagonal of A,
   a. Trace0
   b. Thing
   c. Undefined
   d. Undefined

95. In geographic information systems, a _____ comprises an entity with a geographic location, typically determined by points, arcs, or polygons. Carriageways and cadastres exemplify _____ data.
   a. Thing
   b. Feature0
   c. Undefined
   d. Undefined

96. An _____ is the fee paid on borrow money.
   a. Interest rate0
   b. Concept
   c. Undefined
   d. Undefined

Chapter 4. Systems of Equations and Inequalities

97. In mathematics, there are several meanings of _____ depending on the subject.
   a. Degree0
   b. Thing
   c. Undefined
   d. Undefined

98. In mathematics, the _____ of a function is the set of all "output" values produced by that function. Given a function $f : A \to B$, the _____ of f, is defined to be the set $\{x \in B : x = f(a)$ for some $a \in A\}$.
   a. Range0
   b. Thing
   c. Undefined
   d. Undefined

99. In mathematics, a _____ of a k-place relation $L \subseteq X_1 \times \ldots \times X_k$ is one of the sets X_j, $1 \leq j \leq k$. In the special case where k = 2 and $L \subseteq X_1 \times X_2$ is a function $L : X_1 \to X_2$, it is conventional to refer to X_1 as the _____ of the function and to refer to X_2 as the codomain of the function.
   a. Thing
   b. Domain0
   c. Undefined
   d. Undefined

100. _____ is the middle point of a line segment.
   a. Midpoint0
   b. Thing
   c. Undefined
   d. Undefined

101. _____ is the art and science of designing buildings and structures.
   a. Thing
   b. Architecture0
   c. Undefined
   d. Undefined

102. _____ is the scientific study of celestial objects such as stars, planets, comets, and galaxies; and phenomena that originate outside the Earth's atmosphere.
   a. Thing
   b. Astronomy0
   c. Undefined
   d. Undefined

103. _____ is the design, analysis, and/or construction of works for practical purposes.
   a. Engineering0
   b. Thing
   c. Undefined
   d. Undefined

104. _____ is a set, with some particular properties and usually some additional structure, such as the operations of addition or multiplication, for instance.
   a. Space0
   b. Thing
   c. Undefined
   d. Undefined

105. A _____, as defined by the International Astronomical Union, is a celestial body orbiting a star or stellar remnant that is massive enough to be rounded by its own gravity, not massive enough to cause thermonuclear fusion in its core, and has cleared its neighboring region of planetesimals.
   a. Thing
   b. Planet0
   c. Undefined
   d. Undefined

106. A _____ is a unit of length, usually used to measure distance, in a number of different systems, including Imperial units, United States customary units and Norwegian/Swedish mil. Its size can vary from system to system, but in each is between 1 and 10 kilometers. In contemporary English contexts _____ refers to either:

a. Thing
b. Mile0
c. Undefined
d. Undefined

107. _____ is the estimation of a physical quantity such as distance, energy, temperature, or time.
a. Measurement0
b. Thing
c. Undefined
d. Undefined

108. _____ is a notation for writing numbers that is often used by scientists and mathematicians to make it easier to write large and small numbers.
a. Thing
b. Scientific notation0
c. Undefined
d. Undefined

Chapter 5. Polynomials and Exponents

1. _____ is the transport of people on a trip/journey or the process or time involved in a person or object moving from one location to another.
   - a. Thing
   - b. Travel0
   - c. Undefined
   - d. Undefined

2. In mathematics, a _____ is a particular kind of polynomial, having just one term.
   - a. Thing
   - b. Monomial0
   - c. Undefined
   - d. Undefined

3. _____ is the fee paid on borrowed money.
   - a. Thing
   - b. Interest0
   - c. Undefined
   - d. Undefined

4. In mathematics, a _____ is the result of multiplying, or an expression that identifies factors to be multiplied.
   - a. Thing
   - b. Product0
   - c. Undefined
   - d. Undefined

5. A _____ is a symbolic representation denoting a quantity or expression. It often represents an "unknown" quantity that has the potential to change.
   - a. Variable0
   - b. Thing
   - c. Undefined
   - d. Undefined

6. In mathematics, _____ growth occurs when the growth rate of a function is always proportional to the function's current size.
   - a. Thing
   - b. Exponential0
   - c. Undefined
   - d. Undefined

7. An _____ is a combination of numbers, operators, grouping symbols and/or free variables and bound variables arranged in a meaningful way which can be evaluated..
   - a. Thing
   - b. Expression0
   - c. Undefined
   - d. Undefined

8. A _____ is the result of the addition of a set of numbers. The numbers may be natural numbers, complex numbers, matrices, or still more complicated objects. An infinite _____ is a subtle procedure known as a series.
   - a. Thing
   - b. Sum0
   - c. Undefined
   - d. Undefined

9. _____ is a mathematical operation, written a^n, involving two numbers, the base a and the exponent n.
   - a. Exponentiating0
   - b. Thing
   - c. Undefined
   - d. Undefined

10. _____ is a mathematical operation, written a^n, involving two numbers, the base a and the exponent n.
    - a. Thing
    - b. Exponentiation0
    - c. Undefined
    - d. Undefined

11. In mathematics, there are several meanings of _____ depending on the subject.

Chapter 5. Polynomials and Exponents

    a. Degree0
    b. Thing
    c. Undefined
    d. Undefined

12. In mathematics and the mathematical sciences, a _____ is a fixed, but possibly unspecified, value. This is in contrast to a variable, which is not fixed.
    a. Constant0
    b. Thing
    c. Undefined
    d. Undefined

13. _____ is a fixed, but possibly unspecified, value. This is in contrast to a variable, which is not fixed.
    a. Thing
    b. Constant term0
    c. Undefined
    d. Undefined

14. In mathematics, factorization (British English: factorisation) or factoring is the decomposition of an object (for example, a number, a polynomial, or a matrix) into a product of other objects, or _____, which when multiplied together give the original.
    a. Factors0
    b. Thing
    c. Undefined
    d. Undefined

15. The _____ are the only integral domain whose positive elements are well-ordered, and in which order is preserved by addition. Like the natural numbers, the _____ form a countably infinite set. The set of all _____ is usually denoted in mathematics by a boldface Z .
    a. Integers0
    b. Thing
    c. Undefined
    d. Undefined

16. _____, either of the curved-bracket punctuation marks that together make a set of _____
    a. Parentheses0
    b. Thing
    c. Undefined
    d. Undefined

17. In mathematics, _____ expressions is used to reduce the expression into the lowest possible term.
    a. Simplifying0
    b. Thing
    c. Undefined
    d. Undefined

18. _____ has many meanings, most of which simply .
    a. Thing
    b. Power0
    c. Undefined
    d. Undefined

19. In mathematics, a _____ is the end result of a division problem. It can also be expressed as the number of times the divisor divides into the dividend.
    a. Quotient0
    b. Thing
    c. Undefined
    d. Undefined

20. _____ is the largest positive integer that divides both numbers without remainder.
    a. Thing
    b. Common Factor0
    c. Undefined
    d. Undefined

Chapter 5. Polynomials and Exponents

21. The _____, the average in everyday English, which is also called the arithmetic _____ (and is distinguished from the geometric _____ or harmonic _____). The average is also called the sample _____. The expected value of a random variable, which is also called the population _____.
   a. Thing
   b. Mean0
   c. Undefined
   d. Undefined

22. The plus and _____ signs are mathematical symbols used to represent the notions of positive and negative as well as the operations of addition and subtraction.
   a. Minus0
   b. Thing
   c. Undefined
   d. Undefined

23. Sir Isaac _____, was an English physicist, mathematician, astronomer, natural philosopher, and alchemist, regarded by many as the greatest figure in the history of science
   a. Newton0
   b. Person
   c. Undefined
   d. Undefined

24. Sir _____ was an English physicist, mathematician, astronomer, natural philosopher, and alchemist, regarded by many as the greatest figure in the history of science.
   a. Isaac Newton0
   b. Person
   c. Undefined
   d. Undefined

25. _____ is the design, analysis, and/or construction of works for practical purposes.
   a. Engineering0
   b. Thing
   c. Undefined
   d. Undefined

26. A _____ is a function that assigns a number to subsets of a given set.
   a. Measure0
   b. Thing
   c. Undefined
   d. Undefined

27. In mathematics, an inequality is a statement about the relative size or order of two objects. For example 14 > 10, or 14 is _____ 10.
   a. Thing
   b. Greater than0
   c. Undefined
   d. Undefined

28. Mathematical _____ is used to represent ideas.
   a. Thing
   b. Notation0
   c. Undefined
   d. Undefined

29. The decimal separator is a symbol used to mark the boundary between the integral and the fractional parts of a decimal numeral. Terms implying the symbol used are _____ and decimal comma.
   a. Concept
   b. Decimal point0
   c. Undefined
   d. Undefined

30. The _____ or parallactic second is a unit of length used in astronomy.

a. Parsec0 b. Thing
c. Undefined d. Undefined

31. _____ is a notation for writing numbers that is often used by scientists and mathematicians to make it easier to write large and small numbers.
a. Thing b. Scientific notation0
c. Undefined d. Undefined

32. _____ is the writing of numbers in the base-ten numeral system, which uses various symbols called digits for ten distinct values 0, 1, 2, 3, 4, 5, 6, 7, 8 and 9 to represent numbers
a. Thing b. Decimal notation0
c. Undefined d. Undefined

33. In mathematics, the _____ (or modulus) of a real number is its numerical value without regard to its sign.
a. Absolute value0 b. Thing
c. Undefined d. Undefined

34. A _____ is a deliberate process for transforming one or more inputs into one or more results.
a. Thing b. Calculation0
c. Undefined d. Undefined

35. The _____ in a vacuum is an important physical constant denoted by the letter c for constant or the Latin word celeritas meaning "swiftness
a. Speed of light0 b. Thing
c. Undefined d. Undefined

36. _____ is electromagnetic radiation with a wavelength that is visible to the eye (visible _____) or, in a technical or scientific context, electromagnetic radiation of any wavelength.
a. Light0 b. Thing
c. Undefined d. Undefined

37. _____ or arithmetics is the oldest and most elementary branch of mathematics, used by almost everyone, for tasks ranging from simple daily counting to advanced science and business calculations.
a. Thing b. Arithmetic0
c. Undefined d. Undefined

38. _____, Greek for "knowledge of nature," is the branch of science concerned with the discovery and characterization of universal laws which govern matter, energy, space, and time.
a. Thing b. Physics0
c. Undefined d. Undefined

39. _____ is the property of a physical object that quantifies the amount of matter and energy it is equivalent to.
a. Thing b. Mass0
c. Undefined d. Undefined

Chapter 5. Polynomials and Exponents

40. A _____ is a unit of length, usually used to measure distance, in a number of different systems, including Imperial units, United States customary units and Norwegian/Swedish mil. Its size can vary from system to system, but in each is between 1 and 10 kilometers. In contemporary English contexts _____ refers to either:
   a. Thing
   b. Mile0
   c. Undefined
   d. Undefined

41. In economics _____ means before deductions brutto, e.g. _____ domestic or national product, or _____ profit or income
   a. Thing
   b. Gross0
   c. Undefined
   d. Undefined

42. A _____ is a special kind of ratio, indicating a relationship between two measurements with different units, such as miles to gallons or cents to pounds.
   a. Thing
   b. Rate0
   c. Undefined
   d. Undefined

43. In botany, _____ are above-ground plant organs specialized for photosynthesis. Their characteristics are typically analyzed by using Fiobonacci's sequences.
   a. Thing
   b. Leaves0
   c. Undefined
   d. Undefined

44. In geometry, a _____ (Greek words diairo = divide and metro = measure) of a circle is any straight line segment that passes through the centre and whose endpoints are on the circular boundary, or, in more modern usage, the length of such a line segment. When using the word in the more modern sense, one speaks of the _____ rather than a _____, because all diameters of a circle have the same length. This length is twice the radius. The _____ of a circle is also the longest chord that the circle has.
   a. Diameter0
   b. Thing
   c. Undefined
   d. Undefined

45. In plane geometry, a _____ is a polygon with four equal sides, four right angles, and parallel opposite sides. In algebra, the _____ of a number is that number multiplied by itself.
   a. Square0
   b. Thing
   c. Undefined
   d. Undefined

46. In classical geometry, a _____ of a circle or sphere is any line segment from its center to its boundary. By extension, the _____ of a circle or sphere is the length of any such segment. The _____ is half the diameter. In science and engineering the term _____ of curvature is commonly used as a synonym for _____.
   a. Radius0
   b. Thing
   c. Undefined
   d. Undefined

47. The _____ of a solid object is the three-dimensional concept of how much space it occupies, often quantified numerically.
   a. Volume0
   b. Thing
   c. Undefined
   d. Undefined

Chapter 5. Polynomials and Exponents

48. In mathematics, a _____ is an expression that is constructed from one or more variables and constants, using only the operations of addition, subtraction, multiplication, and constant positive whole number exponents. is a _____. Note in particular that division by an expression containing a variable is not in general allowed in polynomials. [1]
    a. Thing
    b. Polynomial0
    c. Undefined
    d. Undefined

49. A _____ is one of the basic shapes of geometry: a polygon with three vertices and three sides which are straight line segments.
    a. Triangle0
    b. Thing
    c. Undefined
    d. Undefined

50. In geometry, a _____ is defined as a quadrilateral where all four of its angles are right angles.
    a. Thing
    b. Rectangle0
    c. Undefined
    d. Undefined

51. _____ is the distance around a given two-dimensional object. As a general rule, the _____ of a polygon can always be calculated by adding all the length of the sides together. So, the formula for triangles is P = a + b + c, where a, b and c stand for each side of it. For quadrilaterals the equation is P = a + b + c + d. For equilateral polygons, P = na, where n is the number of sides and a is the side length.
    a. Thing
    b. Perimeter0
    c. Undefined
    d. Undefined

52. An _____ triange is a triangle with at least two sides of equal length.
    a. Isosceles0
    b. Thing
    c. Undefined
    d. Undefined

53. The mathematical concept of a _____ expresses the intuitive idea of deterministic dependence between two quantities, one of which is viewed as primary and the other as secondary. A _____ then is a way to associate a unique output for each input of a specified type, for example, a real number or an element of a given set.
    a. Function0
    b. Thing
    c. Undefined
    d. Undefined

54. In elementary algebra, a _____ is a polynomial with two terms: the sum of two monomials. It is the simplest kind of polynomial except for a monomial.
    a. Binomial0
    b. Thing
    c. Undefined
    d. Undefined

55. The _____ is the maximum of the degrees of all terms in the polynomial.
    a. Degree of a polynomial0
    b. Thing
    c. Undefined
    d. Undefined

56. The word _____ comes from the Latin word linearis, which means created by lines.
    a. Thing
    b. Linear0
    c. Undefined
    d. Undefined

Chapter 5. Polynomials and Exponents

57. A _____ is a first degree polynomial mathematical function of the form: f(x) = mx + b where m and b are real constants and x is a real variable.
   a. Linear function0
   b. Thing
   c. Undefined
   d. Undefined

58. A _____ is a polynomial function of the form f(x) = ax^2 + bx +c , where a, b, c are real numbers and a , 0.
   a. Event
   b. Quadratic function0
   c. Undefined
   d. Undefined

59. _____ is a function of the form
   a. Thing
   b. Cubic function0
   c. Undefined
   d. Undefined

60. _____ of an object is its speed in a particular direction.
   a. Thing
   b. Velocity0
   c. Undefined
   d. Undefined

61. In mathematics, a _____ is a constant multiplicative factor of a certain object. The object can be such things as a variable, a vector, a function, etc. For example, the _____ of $9x^2$ is 9.
   a. Thing
   b. Coefficient0
   c. Undefined
   d. Undefined

62. _____ is the symbold used to indicate the nth root of a number
   a. Thing
   b. Radical0
   c. Undefined
   d. Undefined

63. In mathematics, the concept of a _____ tries to capture the intuitive idea of a geometrical one-dimensional and continuous object. A simple example is the circle.
   a. Thing
   b. Curve0
   c. Undefined
   d. Undefined

64. In linear algebra, the _____ of an n-by-n square matrix A is defined to be the sum of the elements on the main diagonal of A,
   a. Trace0
   b. Thing
   c. Undefined
   d. Undefined

65. A _____ is a set of numbers that designate location in a given reference system, such as x,y in a planar _____ system or an x,y,z in a three-dimensional _____ system.
   a. Coordinate0
   b. Thing
   c. Undefined
   d. Undefined

66. In astronomy, geography, geometry and related sciences and contexts, a plane is said to be _____ at a given point if it is locally perpendicular to the gradient of the gravity field, i.e., with the direction of the gravitational force at that point.
   a. Thing
   b. Horizontal0
   c. Undefined
   d. Undefined

Chapter 5. Polynomials and Exponents

67. In mathematics, a matrix can be thought of as each row or _____ being a vector. Hence, a space formed by row vectors or _____ vectors are said to be a row space or a _____ space.
   a. Concept
   b. Column0
   c. Undefined
   d. Undefined

68. _____ element of an element x with respect to a binary operation * with identity element e is an element y such that x * y = y * x = e. In particular,
   a. Thing
   b. Inverse0
   c. Undefined
   d. Undefined

69. In mathematics, the _____ inverse, or opposite, of a number n is the number that, when added to n, yields zero. The _____ inverse of n is denoted −n.
   a. Thing
   b. Additive0
   c. Undefined
   d. Undefined

70. In mathematics, the _____ of a number n is the number that, when added to n, yields zero. The _____ of n is denoted −n. For example, 7 is −7, because 7 + (−7) = 0, and the _____ of −0.3 is 0.3, because −0.3 + 0.3 = 0.
   a. Thing
   b. Additive inverse0
   c. Undefined
   d. Undefined

71. In mathematics, the additive inverse, or _____ of a number n is the number that, when added to n, yields zero. The additive inverse of n is denoted −n. For example, 7 is −7, because 7 + (−7) = 0, and the additive inverse of −0.3 is 0.3, because −0.3 + 0.3 = 0.
   a. Opposite0
   b. Thing
   c. Undefined
   d. Undefined

72. In mathematics, the term _____ is applied to certain functions. There are two common ways it is applied: these are related historically, but diverged somewhat during the twentieth century.
   a. Functional0
   b. Thing
   c. Undefined
   d. Undefined

73. A _____, or Ocean Surface Waves are surface waves that occur in the upper layer of the ocean.
   a. Water wave0
   b. Thing
   c. Undefined
   d. Undefined

74. _____ are activities that are governed by a set of rules or customs and often engaged in competitively.
   a. Sports0
   b. Thing
   c. Undefined
   d. Undefined

75. In geometry, a _____ is a special kind of point, usually a corner of a polygon, polyhedron, or higher dimensional polytope. In the geometry of curves a _____ is a point of where the first derivative of curvature is zero. In graph theory, a _____ is the fundamental unit out of which graphs are formed
   a. Vertex0
   b. Thing
   c. Undefined
   d. Undefined

Chapter 5. Polynomials and Exponents

76. In geometry a _____ is a plane figure that is bounded by a closed path or circuit, composed of a finite number of sequential line segments.
    a. Polygon0
    b. Thing
    c. Undefined
    d. Undefined

77. A _____ can refer to a line joining two nonadjacent vertices of a polygon or polyhedron, or in some contexts any upward or downward sloping line. .
    a. Thing
    b. Diagonal0
    c. Undefined
    d. Undefined

78. In geometry, a _____ is any polygon with ten sides and ten angles, and usually refers to a regular _____, having all sides of equal length and all angles equal to 144¡ã, therefore making each angle of a regular _____ be 144¡ã.
    a. Thing
    b. Decagon0
    c. Undefined
    d. Undefined

79. _____ is a kind of property which exists as magnitude or multitude. It is among the basic classes of things along with quality, substance, change, and relation.
    a. Thing
    b. Amount0
    c. Undefined
    d. Undefined

80. _____ is the middle point of a line segment.
    a. Midpoint0
    b. Thing
    c. Undefined
    d. Undefined

81. _____ are the basic objects of study in graph theory. Informally speaking, a graph is a set of objects called points, nodes, or vertices connected by links called lines or edges.
    a. Thing
    b. Graphs0
    c. Undefined
    d. Undefined

82. Acid _____ ratio measures the ability of a company to use its near cash or quick assets to immediately extinguish its current liabilities.
    a. Test0
    b. Thing
    c. Undefined
    d. Undefined

83. In mathematics, a _____ is a mathematical statement which appears likely to be true, but has not been formally proven to be true under the rules of mathematical logic.
    a. Conjecture0
    b. Concept
    c. Undefined
    d. Undefined

84. Compass and straightedge or ruler-and-compass _____ is the _____ of lengths or angles using only an idealized ruler and compass.
    a. Construction0
    b. Thing
    c. Undefined
    d. Undefined

85. In geometry, the _____ of an object is a point in some sense in the middle of the object.

Chapter 5. Polynomials and Exponents

   a. Thing
   b. Center0
   c. Undefined
   d. Undefined

86. In mathematics, _____ is an elementary arithmetic operation. When one of the numbers is a whole number, _____ is the repeated sum of the other number.
   a. Multiplication0
   b. Thing
   c. Undefined
   d. Undefined

87. _____ is a synonym for information.
   a. Data0
   b. Thing
   c. Undefined
   d. Undefined

88. In mathematics, and in particular in abstract algebra, the _____ is a property of binary operations that generalises the distributive law from elementary algebra.
   a. Thing
   b. Distributive property0
   c. Undefined
   d. Undefined

89. In abstract algebra, _____ consists of sets with binary operations that satisfy certain axioms.
   a. Thing
   b. Grouping0
   c. Undefined
   d. Undefined

90. _____ are objects, characters, or other concrete representations of ideas, concepts, or other abstractions.
   a. Symbols0
   b. Thing
   c. Undefined
   d. Undefined

91. A _____ is a polynomial consisting of three terms; in other words, it is the sum of three monomials.
   a. Thing
   b. Trinomial0
   c. Undefined
   d. Undefined

92. In mathematics, a _____ can mean either an element of the set {1, 2, 3, ...} (i.e the positive integers) or an element of the set {0, 1, 2, 3, ...} (i.e. the non-negative integers).
   a. Concept
   b. Whole number0
   c. Undefined
   d. Undefined

93. A _____ is a three-dimensional solid object bounded by six square faces, facets, or sides, with three meeting at each vertex.
   a. Thing
   b. Cube0
   c. Undefined
   d. Undefined

94. A _____ is a negotiable instrument instructing a financial institution to pay a specific amount of a specific currency from a specific demand account held in the maker/depositor's name with that institution. Both the maker and payee may be natural persons or legal entities.
   a. Check0
   b. Thing
   c. Undefined
   d. Undefined

95. A _____ is the part of the dividend that is left over when the dividend is not evenly divisible by the divisor.

Chapter 5. Polynomials and Exponents

    a. Thing
    c. Undefined
    b. Remainder0
    d. Undefined

96. _____ is a payment made by a company to its shareholders
    a. Thing
    c. Undefined
    b. Dividend0
    d. Undefined

97. In mathematics, a _____ of an integer n, also called a factor of n, is an integer which evenly divides n without leaving a remainder.
    a. Divisor0
    c. Undefined
    b. Thing
    d. Undefined

98. In arithmetic, _____ is a procedure for calculating the division of one integer, called the dividend, by another integer called the divisor, to produce a result called the quotient.
    a. Long division0
    c. Undefined
    b. Thing
    d. Undefined

99. In mathematics, _____ allows the rapid division of any polynomial by a binomial of the form x − r. It was described by Paolo Ruffini in 1809. _____ is a special case of long division when the divisor is a linear factor.
    a. Thing
    c. Undefined
    b. Ruffini's rule0
    d. Undefined

100. _____ in algebra is an application of polynomial long division.
    a. Thing
    c. Undefined
    b. Remainder theorem0
    d. Undefined

101. In mathematics, a _____ is a statement that can be proved on the basis of explicitly stated or previously agreed assumptions.
    a. Theorem0
    c. Undefined
    b. Thing
    d. Undefined

102. In mathematics, _____ is the decomposition of an object into a product of other objects, or factors, which when multiplied together give the original.
    a. Factoring0
    c. Undefined
    b. Thing
    d. Undefined

103. In mathematics, a _____ number (or a _____) is a natural number that has exactly two (distinct) natural number divisors, which are 1 and the _____ number itself.
    a. Prime0
    c. Undefined
    b. Thing
    d. Undefined

104. The term _____ can refer to an integer which is the square of some other integer, or an algebraic expression that can be factored as the square of some other expression.
    a. Thing
    c. Undefined
    b. Perfect square0
    d. Undefined

Chapter 5. Polynomials and Exponents

105. In mathematics, a _____ of a number x is a number r such that r^2 = x, or in words, a number r whose square (the result of multiplying the number by itself) is x.
   a. Square root0
   b. Thing
   c. Undefined
   d. Undefined

106. In mathematics, a _____ of a complex-valued function f is a member x of the domain of f such that f(x) vanishes at x, that is, x : f (x) = 0.
   a. Root0
   b. Thing
   c. Undefined
   d. Undefined

107. _____ are of a number n in its third power-the result of multiplying it by itself three times.
   a. Thing
   b. Cubes0
   c. Undefined
   d. Undefined

108. A _____ is a number which is the cube of an integer.
   a. Perfect cube0
   b. Thing
   c. Undefined
   d. Undefined

109. A _____ of a number is a number a such that a^3 = x.
   a. Cube root0
   b. Thing
   c. Undefined
   d. Undefined

110. The _____ of a positive integer are the prime numbers that divide into that integer exactly, without leaving a remainder. The process of finding these numbers is called integer factorization, or prime factorization.
   a. Thing
   b. Prime factor0
   c. Undefined
   d. Undefined

111. In mathematics, a _____ can mean either an element of the set {1, 2, 3, ...} (i.e the positive integers or the counting numbers) or an element of the set {0, 1, 2, 3, ...} (i.e. the non-negative integers).
   a. Natural number0
   b. Thing
   c. Undefined
   d. Undefined

112. A _____ signifies a point or points of probability on a subject e.g., the _____ of creativity, which allows for the formation of rule or norm or law by interpretation of the phenomena events that can be created.
   a. Thing
   b. Principle0
   c. Undefined
   d. Undefined

113. In mathematics, a _____ is a polynomial equation of the second degree. The general form is ax^2 + bx +c = 0.
   a. Quadratic equation0
   b. Thing
   c. Undefined
   d. Undefined

114. An _____ or member of a set is an object that when collected together make up the set.
   a. Element0
   b. Thing
   c. Undefined
   d. Undefined

Chapter 5. Polynomials and Exponents

115. In mathematics, the _____ , or members of a set or more generally a class are all those objects which when collected together make up the set or class.
   a. Elements0
   b. Thing
   c. Undefined
   d. Undefined

116. In mathematics, the _____ of a function is the set of all "output" values produced by that function. Given a function $f : A \to B$, the _____ of f, is defined to be the set $\{x \in B : x = f(a) \text{ for some } a \in A\}$.
   a. Range0
   b. Thing
   c. Undefined
   d. Undefined

117. In mathematics, a _____ of a k-place relation $L \subseteq X_1 \times \ldots \times X_k$ is one of the sets X_j, $1 \leq j \leq k$. In the special case where k = 2 and $L \subseteq X_1 \times X_2$ is a function $L : X_1 \to X_2$, it is conventional to refer to X_1 as the _____ of the function and to refer to X_2 as the codomain of the function.
   a. Thing
   b. Domain0
   c. Undefined
   d. Undefined

118. An _____ is a collection of two not necessarily distinct objects, one of which is distinguished as the first coordinate and the other as the second coordinate.
   a. Thing
   b. Ordered pair0
   c. Undefined
   d. Undefined

119. In mathematics, the conjugate _____ or adjoint matrix of an m-by-n matrix A with complex entries is the n-by-m matrix A* obtained from A by taking the transpose and then taking the complex conjugate of each entry.
   a. Pairs0
   b. Thing
   c. Undefined
   d. Undefined

120. _____ means in succession or back-to-back
   a. Consecutive0
   b. Thing
   c. Undefined
   d. Undefined

121. _____ is a set, with some particular properties and usually some additional structure, such as the operations of addition or multiplication, for instance.
   a. Space0
   b. Thing
   c. Undefined
   d. Undefined

122. A _____ is a vehicle, missile or aircraft which obtains thrust by the reaction to the ejection of fast moving fluid from within a _____ engine.
   a. Rocket0
   b. Thing
   c. Undefined
   d. Undefined

123. _____ is defined as the rate of change or derivative with respect to time of velocity.
   a. Thing
   b. Acceleration0
   c. Undefined
   d. Undefined

124. The metre (or _____, see spelling differences) is a measure of length. It is the basic unit of length in the metric system and in the International System of Units (SI), used around the world for general and scientific purposes.

Chapter 5. Polynomials and Exponents

a. Concept
b. Meter0
c. Undefined
d. Undefined

125. Initial objects are also called _____, and terminal objects are also called final.
 a. Coterminal0
 b. Thing
 c. Undefined
 d. Undefined

126. In mathematics and more specifically set theory, the _____ set is the unique set which contains no elements.
 a. Empty0
 b. Thing
 c. Undefined
 d. Undefined

127. _____ forms part of thinking. Considered the most complex of all intellectual functions, _____ has been defined as higher-order cognitive process that requires the modulation and control of more routine or fundamental skills.
 a. Thing
 b. Problem solving0
 c. Undefined
 d. Undefined

128. In logic, and especially in its applications to mathematics and philosophy, a _____ is an exception to a proposed general rule, i.e., a specific instance of the falsity of a universal quantification (a "for all" statement).
 a. Thing
 b. Counterexample0
 c. Undefined
 d. Undefined

129. _____ is a natural number that has exactly two distinct natural number divisors, which are 1 and the _____ itself.
 a. Thing
 b. Prime number0
 c. Undefined
 d. Undefined

130. A frame of _____ is a particular perspective from which the universe is observed.
 a. Thing
 b. Reference0
 c. Undefined
 d. Undefined

131. In mathematics, a _____ may be described informally as a number that can be given by an infinite decimal representation.
 a. Thing
 b. Real number0
 c. Undefined
 d. Undefined

132. In mathematics, an _____ number is any real number that is not a rational number- that is, it is a number which cannot be expressed as a fraction m/n, where m and n are integers.
 a. Thing
 b. Irrational0
 c. Undefined
 d. Undefined

133. In mathematics, an _____ is any real number that is not a rational number ¡[a] that is, it is a number which cannot be expressed as m/n, where m and n are integers.
 a. Irrational number0
 b. Thing
 c. Undefined
 d. Undefined

Chapter 5. Polynomials and Exponents

134. In mathematics, _____ are any real number that is not a rational number ¡ª that is, it is a number which cannot be expressed as m/n, where m and n are integers.
- a. Thing
- b. Irrational numbers0
- c. Undefined
- d. Undefined

135. In geometry, a line _____ is a part of a line that is bounded by two end points, and contains every point on the line between its end points.
- a. Segment0
- b. Concept
- c. Undefined
- d. Undefined

136. A _____ is a part of a line that is bounded by two end points, and contains every point on the line between its end points.
- a. Line segment0
- b. Thing
- c. Undefined
- d. Undefined

137. Three or more points that lie on the same line are called _____.
- a. Thing
- b. Collinear0
- c. Undefined
- d. Undefined

138. In mathematics, a _____ is a two-dimensional manifold or surface that is perfectly flat.
- a. Plane0
- b. Thing
- c. Undefined
- d. Undefined

139. In arithmetic and algebra, when a number or expression is both preceded and followed by a binary operation, an _____ is required for which operation should be applied first.
- a. Order of operations0
- b. Thing
- c. Undefined
- d. Undefined

140. Mathematical _____ really refers to two distinct areas of research: the first is the application of the techniques of formal _____ to mathematics and mathematical reasoning, and the second, in the other direction, the application of mathematical techniques to the representation and analysis of formal _____.
- a. Thing
- b. Logic0
- c. Undefined
- d. Undefined

141. In mathematics, a _____ is an n-tuple with n being 3.
- a. Thing
- b. Triple0
- c. Undefined
- d. Undefined

142. _____ is a relation in Euclidean geometry among the three sides of a right triangle.
- a. Pythagorean Theorem0
- b. Thing
- c. Undefined
- d. Undefined

143. In a right triangle, the _____ of the triangle are the two sides that are perpendicular to each other, as opposed to the hypotenuse.

Chapter 5. Polynomials and Exponents

a. Thing
b. Legs0
c. Undefined
d. Undefined

144. The _____ of a right triangle is the triangle's longest side; the side opposite the right angle.
    a. Thing
    b. Hypotenuse0
    c. Undefined
    d. Undefined

145. _____ has one 90° internal angle a right angle.
    a. Right triangle0
    b. Thing
    c. Undefined
    d. Undefined

146. A _____ is a method for fastening or securing linear material such as rope by tying or interweaving. It may consist of a length of one or more segments of rope, string, webbing, twine, strap or even chain interwoven so as to create in the line the ability to bind to itself or to some other object - the "load". Knots have been the subject of interest both for their ancient origins, common use, and the mathematical implications of _____ theory.
    a. Knot0
    b. Thing
    c. Undefined
    d. Undefined

147. The _____ of measurement are a globally standardized and modernized form of the metric system.
    a. Units0
    b. Thing
    c. Undefined
    d. Undefined

148. _____ is the estimation of a physical quantity such as distance, energy, temperature, or time.
    a. Measurement0
    b. Thing
    c. Undefined
    d. Undefined

149. The _____ is a unit of length nearly equal to the semi-major axis of Earth's orbit around the Sun. The currently accepted value of the AU is 149 597 870 691 ± 30 metres.
    a. Thing
    b. Astronomical unit0
    c. Undefined
    d. Undefined

150. In mathematics, an _____, mean, or central tendency of a data set refers to a measure of the "middle" or "expected" value of the data set.
    a. Average0
    b. Concept
    c. Undefined
    d. Undefined

151. A _____ given two distinct points A and B on the _____, is the set of points C on the line containing points A and B such that A is not strictly between C and B.
    a. Thing
    b. Ray0
    c. Undefined
    d. Undefined

152. In _____ algebra, a *-ring is an associative ring with an antilinear, antiautomorphism * : A ¨ A which is an involution.
    a. Star0
    b. Thing
    c. Undefined
    d. Undefined

Chapter 5. Polynomials and Exponents

153. A _____, as defined by the International Astronomical Union, is a celestial body orbiting a star or stellar remnant that is massive enough to be rounded by its own gravity, not massive enough to cause thermonuclear fusion in its core, and has cleared its neighboring region of planetesimals.
    a. Planet0
    b. Thing
    c. Undefined
    d. Undefined

154. Order theory is a branch of mathematics that studies various kinds of binary relations that capture the intuitive notion of a mathematical _____.
    a. Thing
    b. Ordering0
    c. Undefined
    d. Undefined

155. In physics, an _____ is the path that an object makes around another object while under the influence of a source of centripetal force, such as gravity.
    a. Orbit0
    b. Thing
    c. Undefined
    d. Undefined

156. _____ is often used to describe the measurement of the steepness, incline, gradient, or grade of a straight line. The _____ is defined as the ratio of the "rise" divided by the "run" between two points on a line, or in other words, the ratio of the altitude change to the horizontal distance between any two points on the line.
    a. Slope0
    b. Thing
    c. Undefined
    d. Undefined

157. In common philosophical language, a proposition or _____, is the content of an assertion, that is, it is true-or-false and defined by the meaning of a particular piece of language.
    a. Statement0
    b. Concept
    c. Undefined
    d. Undefined

158. In geometry, two lines or planes if one falls on the other in such a way as to create congruent adjacent angles. The term may be used as a noun or adjective. Thus, referring to Figure 1, the line AB is the _____ to CD through the point B.
    a. Perpendicular0
    b. Thing
    c. Undefined
    d. Undefined

159. _____ is the difference of electrical potential between two points of an electrical or electronic circuit, expressed in volts
    a. Thing
    b. Voltage0
    c. Undefined
    d. Undefined

160. _____ is the art and science of designing buildings and structures.
    a. Thing
    b. Architecture0
    c. Undefined
    d. Undefined

161. A _____ is a type of debt. All material things can be lent but this article focuses exclusively on monetary loans. Like all debt instruments, a _____ entails the redistribution of financial assets over time, between the lender and the borrower.

a. Loan0   b. Thing
c. Undefined   d. Undefined

162. _____ is the level of functional and/or metabolic efficiency of an organism at both the micro level.
a. Thing   b. Health0
c. Undefined   d. Undefined

163. _____ is the application of tools and a processing medium to the transformation of raw materials into finished goods for sale.
a. Thing   b. Manufacturing0
c. Undefined   d. Undefined

164. _____ is the process of recording pictures by means of capturing light on a light-sensitive medium, such as a film or sensor.
a. Photography0   b. Thing
c. Undefined   d. Undefined

165. In chemistry, a _____ is substance made by combining two or more different materials in such a way that no chemical reaction occurs.
a. Thing   b. Mixture0
c. Undefined   d. Undefined

Chapter 6. Rational Expressions

1. In mathematics, the additive inverse, or _____ of a number n is the number that, when added to n, yields zero. The additive inverse of n is denoted −n. For example, 7 is −7, because 7 + (−7) = 0, and the additive inverse of −0.3 is 0.3, because −0.3 + 0.3 = 0.
   a. Thing
   b. Opposite0
   c. Undefined
   d. Undefined

2. In mathematics, a _____ is a two-dimensional manifold or surface that is perfectly flat.
   a. Thing
   b. Plane0
   c. Undefined
   d. Undefined

3. In mathematics, _____ are two-dimensional manifolds or surfaces that are perfectly flat.
   a. Thing
   b. Planes0
   c. Undefined
   d. Undefined

4. In mathematics, the _____ of a number n is the number that, when added to n, yields zero. The _____ of n is denoted −n. For example, 7 is −7, because 7 + (−7) = 0, and the _____ of −0.3 is 0.3, because −0.3 + 0.3 = 0.
   a. Thing
   b. Additive inverse0
   c. Undefined
   d. Undefined

5. A _____ is a numeral used to indicate a count. The most common use of the word today is to name the part of a fraction that tells the number or count of equal parts.
   a. Thing
   b. Numerator0
   c. Undefined
   d. Undefined

6. In mathematics, a _____ number is a number which can be expressed as a ratio of two integers. Non-integer _____ numbers (commonly called fractions) are usually written as the vulgar fraction a / b, where b is not zero.
   a. Thing
   b. Rational0
   c. Undefined
   d. Undefined

7. In mathematics, a _____ is any function which can be written as the ratio of two polynomial functions.
   a. Rational function0
   b. Thing
   c. Undefined
   d. Undefined

8. An _____ is a combination of numbers, operators, grouping symbols and/or free variables and bound variables arranged in a meaningful way which can be evaluated..
   a. Thing
   b. Expression0
   c. Undefined
   d. Undefined

9. In mathematics, a _____ is an expression that is constructed from one or more variables and constants, using only the operations of addition, subtraction, multiplication, and constant positive whole number exponents. is a _____. Note in particular that division by an expression containing a variable is not in general allowed in polynomials. [1]
   a. Polynomial0
   b. Thing
   c. Undefined
   d. Undefined

10. A _____ is the part of a fraction that tells how many equal parts make up a whole, and which is used in the name of the fraction: "halves", "thirds", "fourths" or "quarters", "fifths" and so on.

Chapter 6. Rational Expressions

a. Denominator0
b. Concept
c. Undefined
d. Undefined

11. The mathematical concept of a _____ expresses the intuitive idea of deterministic dependence between two quantities, one of which is viewed as primary and the other as secondary. A _____ then is a way to associate a unique output for each input of a specified type, for example, a real number or an element of a given set.
    a. Function0
    b. Thing
    c. Undefined
    d. Undefined

12. In mathematics, a _____ of a k-place relation $L \subseteq X_1 \times ... \times X_k$ is one of the sets X_j, $1 \leq j \leq k$. In the special case where k = 2 and $L \subseteq X_1 \times X_2$ is a function $L : X_1 \to X_2$, it is conventional to refer to X_1 as the _____ of the function and to refer to X_2 as the codomain of the function.
    a. Thing
    b. Domain0
    c. Undefined
    d. Undefined

13. A _____ is a symbolic representation denoting a quantity or expression. It often represents an "unknown" quantity that has the potential to change.
    a. Thing
    b. Variable0
    c. Undefined
    d. Undefined

14. A _____ signifies a point or points of probability on a subject e.g., the _____ of creativity, which allows for the formation of rule or norm or law by interpretation of the phenomena events that can be created.
    a. Thing
    b. Principle0
    c. Undefined
    d. Undefined

15. In mathematics, a _____ is the result of multiplying, or an expression that identifies factors to be multiplied.
    a. Product0
    b. Thing
    c. Undefined
    d. Undefined

16. In mathematics, factorization (British English: factorisation) or factoring is the decomposition of an object (for example, a number, a polynomial, or a matrix) into a product of other objects, or _____, which when multiplied together give the original.
    a. Thing
    b. Factors0
    c. Undefined
    d. Undefined

17. The _____ are the only integral domain whose positive elements are well-ordered, and in which order is preserved by addition. Like the natural numbers, the _____ form a countably infinite set. The set of all _____ is usually denoted in mathematics by a boldface Z .
    a. Integers0
    b. Thing
    c. Undefined
    d. Undefined

18. In mathematics, a _____ may be described informally as a number that can be given by an infinite decimal representation.
    a. Thing
    b. Real number0
    c. Undefined
    d. Undefined

Chapter 6. Rational Expressions

19. In mathematics, _____ is an elementary arithmetic operation. When one of the numbers is a whole number, _____ is the repeated sum of the other number.
    a. Thing
    b. Multiplication0
    c. Undefined
    d. Undefined

20. _____ is the largest positive integer that divides both numbers without remainder.
    a. Common Factor0
    b. Thing
    c. Undefined
    d. Undefined

21. In mathematics, _____ expressions is used to reduce the expression into the lowest possible term.
    a. Simplifying0
    b. Thing
    c. Undefined
    d. Undefined

22. In geometry and physics, _____ are half-lines that continue forever in one direction.
    a. Thing
    b. Rays0
    c. Undefined
    d. Undefined

23. _____ is electromagnetic radiation with a wavelength that is visible to the eye (visible _____) or, in a technical or scientific context, electromagnetic radiation of any wavelength.
    a. Thing
    b. Light0
    c. Undefined
    d. Undefined

24. _____ is the process of recording pictures by means of capturing light on a light-sensitive medium, such as a film or sensor.
    a. Thing
    b. Photography0
    c. Undefined
    d. Undefined

25. In mathematics and the mathematical sciences, a _____ is a fixed, but possibly unspecified, value. This is in contrast to a variable, which is not fixed.
    a. Thing
    b. Constant0
    c. Undefined
    d. Undefined

26. Mathematical _____ is used to represent ideas.
    a. Notation0
    b. Thing
    c. Undefined
    d. Undefined

27. A _____ is a set of numbers that designate location in a given reference system, such as x,y in a planar _____ system or an x,y,z in a three-dimensional _____ system.
    a. Coordinate0
    b. Thing
    c. Undefined
    d. Undefined

28. In mathematics, the _____ of a function is the set of all "output" values produced by that function. Given a function $f : A \to B$, the _____ of f, is defined to be the set $\{x \in B : x = f(a) \text{ for some } a \in A\}$.
    a. Thing
    b. Range0
    c. Undefined
    d. Undefined

Chapter 6. Rational Expressions

29. In mathematics, _____ is the decomposition of an object into a product of other objects, or factors, which when multiplied together give the original.
    a. Factoring0
    b. Thing
    c. Undefined
    d. Undefined

30. In mathematics, the multiplicative inverse of a number x, denoted 1/x or x^{-1}, is the number which, when multiplied by x, yields 1. The multiplicative inverse of x is also called the _____ of x.
    a. Reciprocal0
    b. Thing
    c. Undefined
    d. Undefined

31. In mathematics, a _____ of an integer n, also called a factor of n, is an integer which evenly divides n without leaving a remainder.
    a. Divisor0
    b. Thing
    c. Undefined
    d. Undefined

32. A _____ is the result of the addition of a set of numbers. The numbers may be natural numbers, complex numbers, matrices, or still more complicated objects. An infinite _____ is a subtle procedure known as a series.
    a. Sum0
    b. Thing
    c. Undefined
    d. Undefined

33. In mathematics, a _____ is a constant multiplicative factor of a certain object. The object can be such things as a variable, a vector, a function, etc. For example, the _____ of $9x^2$ is 9.
    a. Coefficient0
    b. Thing
    c. Undefined
    d. Undefined

34. In mathematics, a _____ is a number which can be expressed as a ratio of two integers. Non-integer rational numbers (commonly called fractions) are usually written as the vulgar fraction a / b, where b is not zero.
    a. Concept
    b. Rational Number0
    c. Undefined
    d. Undefined

35. _____ is a kind of property which exists as magnitude or multitude. It is among the basic classes of things along with quality, substance, change, and relation.
    a. Amount0
    b. Thing
    c. Undefined
    d. Undefined

36. In classical geometry, a _____ of a circle or sphere is any line segment from its center to its boundary. By extension, the _____ of a circle or sphere is the length of any such segment. The _____ is half the diameter. In science and engineering the term _____ of curvature is commonly used as a synonym for _____.
    a. Radius0
    b. Thing
    c. Undefined
    d. Undefined

37. In plane geometry, a _____ is a polygon with four equal sides, four right angles, and parallel opposite sides. In algebra, the _____ of a number is that number multiplied by itself.
    a. Square0
    b. Thing
    c. Undefined
    d. Undefined

38. _____ is the application of tools and a processing medium to the transformation of raw materials into finished goods for sale.
- a. Manufacturing0
- b. Thing
- c. Undefined
- d. Undefined

39. _____ means in succession or back-to-back
- a. Consecutive0
- b. Thing
- c. Undefined
- d. Undefined

40. A _____ is a special kind of ratio, indicating a relationship between two measurements with different units, such as miles to gallons or cents to pounds.
- a. Rate0
- b. Thing
- c. Undefined
- d. Undefined

41. A _____ is a type of debt. All material things can be lent but this article focuses exclusively on monetary loans. Like all debt instruments, a _____ entails the redistribution of financial assets over time, between the lender and the borrower.
- a. Thing
- b. Loan0
- c. Undefined
- d. Undefined

42. _____ is the fee paid on borrowed money.
- a. Interest0
- b. Thing
- c. Undefined
- d. Undefined

43. An _____ is the fee paid on borrow money.
- a. Concept
- b. Interest rate0
- c. Undefined
- d. Undefined

44. A _____ is a negotiable instrument instructing a financial institution to pay a specific amount of a specific currency from a specific demand account held in the maker/depositor's name with that institution. Both the maker and payee may be natural persons or legal entities.
- a. Thing
- b. Check0
- c. Undefined
- d. Undefined

45. _____ is the transport of people on a trip/journey or the process or time involved in a person or object moving from one location to another.
- a. Thing
- b. Travel0
- c. Undefined
- d. Undefined

46. The _____, the average in everyday English, which is also called the arithmetic _____ (and is distinguished from the geometric _____ or harmonic _____). The average is also called the sample _____. The expected value of a random variable, which is also called the population _____.
- a. Mean0
- b. Thing
- c. Undefined
- d. Undefined

47. A _____ is a landform that extends above the surrounding terrain in a limited area. A _____ is generally steeper than a hill, but there is no universally accepted standard definition for the height of a _____ or a hill although a _____ usually has an identifiable summit.
   a. Thing
   b. Mountain0
   c. Undefined
   d. Undefined

48. In mathematics, an inequality is a statement about the relative size or order of two objects. For example 14 > 10, or 14 is _____ 10.
   a. Greater than0
   b. Thing
   c. Undefined
   d. Undefined

49. Equivalence is the condition of being _____ or essentially equal.
   a. Thing
   b. Equivalent0
   c. Undefined
   d. Undefined

50. _____ is a synonym for information.
   a. Data0
   b. Thing
   c. Undefined
   d. Undefined

51. U.S. liquid _____ is legally defined as 231 cubic inches, and is equal to 3.785411784 litres or abotu 0.13368 cubic feet. This is the most common definition of a _____. The U.S. fluid ounce is defined as 1/128 of a U.S. _____.
   a. Thing
   b. Gallon0
   c. Undefined
   d. Undefined

52. In a company, _____ is the sum of all financial records of salaries, wages, bonuses, and deductions.
   a. Thing
   b. Payroll0
   c. Undefined
   d. Undefined

53. _____ are a measure of time.
   a. Thing
   b. Minutes0
   c. Undefined
   d. Undefined

54. A _____ is a numerical performance objective.
   a. Thing
   b. Quota0
   c. Undefined
   d. Undefined

55. A _____ is 360° or 2∂ radians.
   a. Turn0
   b. Thing
   c. Undefined
   d. Undefined

56. In botany, _____ are above-ground plant organs specialized for photosynthesis. Their characteristics are typically analyzed by using Fiobonacci's sequences.
   a. Leaves0
   b. Thing
   c. Undefined
   d. Undefined

Chapter 6. Rational Expressions

57. _____, in law and economics, is a form of risk management primarily used to hedge against the risk of a contingent loss.
   a. Thing
   b. Insurance0
   c. Undefined
   d. Undefined

58. Regrouping is the act of putting ones into groups of 10. For example, the 1 on the far right of 131 would be denoted _____ if the digit of the number being subtracted is larger than 1, such as 131-99.
   a. Thing
   b. By 100
   c. Undefined
   d. Undefined

59. _____ (or proportionality) are two quantities that vary in such a way that one of the quatities is a constant multiple of the other, or equivalently if they have a constant ratio.
   a. Proportions0
   b. Thing
   c. Undefined
   d. Undefined

60. The _____ of measurement are a globally standardized and modernized form of the metric system.
   a. Units0
   b. Thing
   c. Undefined
   d. Undefined

61. A _____ is a unit of length, usually used to measure distance, in a number of different systems, including Imperial units, United States customary units and Norwegian/Swedish mil. Its size can vary from system to system, but in each is between 1 and 10 kilometers. In contemporary English contexts _____ refers to either:
   a. Mile0
   b. Thing
   c. Undefined
   d. Undefined

62. In mathematics, a _____ is the end result of a division problem. It can also be expressed as the number of times the divisor divides into the dividend.
   a. Thing
   b. Quotient0
   c. Undefined
   d. Undefined

63. A _____ is a quantity that denotes the proportional amount or magnitude of one quantity relative to another.
   a. Ratio0
   b. Thing
   c. Undefined
   d. Undefined

64. A _____ is a compensation which workers receive in exchange for their labor.
   a. Wage0
   b. Thing
   c. Undefined
   d. Undefined

65. _____ is a special mathematical relationship between two quantities. Two quantities are called proportional if they vary in such a way that one of the quantities is a constant multiple of the other, or equivalently if they have a constant ratio.
   a. Thing
   b. Proportionality0
   c. Undefined
   d. Undefined

66. In mathematics, _____ are essentially word problems that are designed to use mathematical critical thinking in everyday situations.

Chapter 6. Rational Expressions

    a. Thing
    c. Undefined
    b. Application problems0
    d. Undefined

67. A _____ is a consumption tax charged at the point of purchase for certain goods and services.
    a. Thing
    c. Undefined
    b. Sales tax0
    d. Undefined

68. In mathematics and logic, a _____ proof is a way of showing the truth or falsehood of a given statement by a straightforward combination of established facts, usually existing lemmas and theorems, without making any further assumptions.
    a. Thing
    c. Undefined
    b. Direct0
    d. Undefined

69. _____ is the relationship between two variables, like a ratio in which the two quantities being compared are different units.
    a. Direct variation0
    c. Undefined
    b. Thing
    d. Undefined

70. In mathematics, two quantities are called _____ if they vary in such a way that one of the quantities is a constant multiple of the other, or equivalently if they have a constant ratio.
    a. Proportional0
    c. Undefined
    b. Thing
    d. Undefined

71. In Euclidean geometry, a _____ is the set of all points in a plane at a fixed distance, called the radius, from a given point, the center.
    a. Thing
    c. Undefined
    b. Circle0
    d. Undefined

72. The _____ is the distance around a closed curve. _____ is a kind of perimeter.
    a. Circumference0
    c. Undefined
    b. Thing
    d. Undefined

73. In geometry, a _____ (Greek words diairo = divide and metro = measure) of a circle is any straight line segment that passes through the centre and whose endpoints are on the circular boundary, or, in more modern usage, the length of such a line segment. When using the word in the more modern sense, one speaks of the _____ rather than a _____, because all diameters of a circle have the same length. This length is twice the radius. The _____ of a circle is also the longest chord that the circle has.
    a. Diameter0
    c. Undefined
    b. Thing
    d. Undefined

74. _____ is a reaction force applied by a stretched string on the objects which stretch it.
    a. Tension0
    c. Undefined
    b. Thing
    d. Undefined

75. _____ is a relationship among three or more variables in which each pair of variables varies directly or inversely.

Chapter 6. Rational Expressions

    a. Joint variation0   b. Thing
    c. Undefined   d. Undefined

76. A _____ is one of the basic shapes of geometry: a polygon with three vertices and three sides which are straight line segments.
    a. Thing   b. Triangle0
    c. Undefined   d. Undefined

77. _____ element of an element x with respect to a binary operation * with identity element e is an element y such that $x * y = y * x = e$. In particular,
    a. Inverse0   b. Thing
    c. Undefined   d. Undefined

78. The _____ of a solid object is the three-dimensional concept of how much space it occupies, often quantified numerically.
    a. Thing   b. Volume0
    c. Undefined   d. Undefined

79. _____ is a physical property of a system that underlies the common notions of hot and cold; something that is hotter has the greater _____.
    a. Thing   b. Temperature0
    c. Undefined   d. Undefined

80. In geometry, a _____ is defined as a quadrilateral where all four of its angles are right angles.
    a. Rectangle0   b. Thing
    c. Undefined   d. Undefined

81. _____ refers to all non-domesticated plants, animals, and other organisms.
    a. Wildlife0   b. Thing
    c. Undefined   d. Undefined

82. _____ is the art and science of designing buildings and structures.
    a. Thing   b. Architecture0
    c. Undefined   d. Undefined

83. _____ is a set, with some particular properties and usually some additional structure, such as the operations of addition or multiplication, for instance.
    a. Space0   b. Thing
    c. Undefined   d. Undefined

84. Compass and straightedge or ruler-and-compass _____ is the _____ of lengths or angles using only an idealized ruler and compass.
    a. Construction0   b. Thing
    c. Undefined   d. Undefined

85. _____ is the level of functional and/or metabolic efficiency of an organism at both the micro level.

Chapter 6. Rational Expressions

    a. Health0
    b. Thing
    c. Undefined
    d. Undefined

86. _____, Greek for "knowledge of nature," is the branch of science concerned with the discovery and characterization of universal laws which govern matter, energy, space, and time.
    a. Thing
    b. Physics0
    c. Undefined
    d. Undefined

87. A _____ is a function that assigns a number to subsets of a given set.
    a. Measure0
    b. Thing
    c. Undefined
    d. Undefined

88. In Euclidean geometry, a uniform _____ is a linear transformation that enlargers or diminishes objects, and whose _____ factor is the same in all directions. This is also called homothethy.
    a. Scale0
    b. Thing
    c. Undefined
    d. Undefined

89. In physics, _____ is an influence that may cause an object to accelerate. It may be experienced as a lift, a push, or a pull. The actual acceleration of the body is determined by the vector sum of all forces acting on it, known as net _____ or resultant _____.
    a. Thing
    b. Force0
    c. Undefined
    d. Undefined

90. In mathematics, a _____ of a number x is a number r such that $r^2 = x$, or in words, a number r whose square (the result of multiplying the number by itself) is x.
    a. Thing
    b. Square root0
    c. Undefined
    d. Undefined

91. A _____ is an object that is attached to a pivot point so that it can swing freely.
    a. Pendulum0
    b. Thing
    c. Undefined
    d. Undefined

92. In business, particularly accounting, a _____ is the time intervals that the accounts, statement, payments, or other calculations cover.
    a. Period0
    b. Thing
    c. Undefined
    d. Undefined

93. In mathematics, a _____ of a complex-valued function f is a member x of the domain of f such that f(x) vanishes at x, that is, x : f (x) = 0.
    a. Thing
    b. Root0
    c. Undefined
    d. Undefined

94. _____ is mass m per unit volume V.
    a. Density0
    b. Thing
    c. Undefined
    d. Undefined

Chapter 6. Rational Expressions

95. _____ is the difference of electrical potential between two points of an electrical or electronic circuit, expressed in volts
   a. Thing
   b. Voltage0
   c. Undefined
   d. Undefined

96. Multiple Signal Classification, also known as _____, is an algorithm used for frequency estimation and emitter location.
   a. Music0
   b. Thing
   c. Undefined
   d. Undefined

97. In statistics the _____ of an event i is the number n_i of times the event occurred in the experiment or the study. These frequencies are often graphically represented in histograms.
   a. Frequency0
   b. Concept
   c. Undefined
   d. Undefined

98. _____ of an object is its speed in a particular direction.
   a. Velocity0
   b. Thing
   c. Undefined
   d. Undefined

99. _____ has many meanings, most of which simply .
   a. Thing
   b. Power0
   c. Undefined
   d. Undefined

100. In mathematics, an _____, mean, or central tendency of a data set refers to a measure of the "middle" or "expected" value of the data set.
   a. Concept
   b. Average0
   c. Undefined
   d. Undefined

101. In acoustics and telecommunication, the _____ of a wave is a component frequency of the signal that is an integer multiple of the fundamental frequency.
   a. Harmonic0
   b. Thing
   c. Undefined
   d. Undefined

102. The _____ is one of several kinds of average. It is the number of variables divided by the sum of the reciprocals of the variables.
   a. Thing
   b. Harmonic mean0
   c. Undefined
   d. Undefined

103. A _____ is an individual or company including a corporation that legally owns one or more shares of stock in a joint stock company.
   a. Stockholder0
   b. Thing
   c. Undefined
   d. Undefined

104. In the most general sense, a _____ is anything that is a hindrance, or puts individuals at a disadvantage.

Chapter 6. Rational Expressions

a. Liability0
b. Thing
c. Undefined
d. Undefined

105. _____ is a way of expressing a number as a fraction of 100 per cent meaning "per hundred".
   a. Thing
   b. Percent0
   c. Undefined
   d. Undefined

106. Acid _____ ratio measures the ability of a company to use its near cash or quick assets to immediately extinguish its current liabilities.
   a. Thing
   b. Test0
   c. Undefined
   d. Undefined

107. _____ is the estimation of a physical quantity such as distance, energy, temperature, or time.
   a. Measurement0
   b. Thing
   c. Undefined
   d. Undefined

108. _____, either of the curved-bracket punctuation marks that together make a set of _____
   a. Parentheses0
   b. Thing
   c. Undefined
   d. Undefined

109. In mathematics, and in particular in abstract algebra, the _____ is a property of binary operations that generalises the distributive law from elementary algebra.
   a. Distributive property0
   b. Thing
   c. Undefined
   d. Undefined

110. _____ is a concept in traditional logic referring to a "type of immediate inference in which from a given proposition another proposition is inferred which has as its subject the predicate of the original proposition and as its predicate the subject of the original proposition (the quality of the proposition being retained)."
   a. Conversion0
   b. Concept
   c. Undefined
   d. Undefined

111. _____ forms part of thinking. Considered the most complex of all intellectual functions, _____ has been defined as higher-order cognitive process that requires the modulation and control of more routine or fundamental skills.
   a. Thing
   b. Problem solving0
   c. Undefined
   d. Undefined

112. In logic and mathematics, logical _____ is a logical relation that holds between a set T of formulas and a formula B when every model (or interpretation or valuation) of T is also a model of B.
   a. Implication0
   b. Concept
   c. Undefined
   d. Undefined

113. A _____ is the second half of a hypothetical proposition. In the standard form of such a proposition, it is the part that follows "then".
   a. Consequent0
   b. Thing
   c. Undefined
   d. Undefined

Chapter 6. Rational Expressions

114. Contraposition is the concept of how two qualities or statements relate to each other. In mathematics, in a statement "if P then Q" for any two propositions P and Q, then the converse is "if Q then P", the inverse is "if not P then not Q", and the _____ is "if not Q then not P".
- a. Thing
- b. Contrapositive0
- c. Undefined
- d. Undefined

115. Mathematical _____ really refers to two distinct areas of research: the first is the application of the techniques of formal _____ to mathematics and mathematical reasoning, and the second, in the other direction, the application of mathematical techniques to the representation and analysis of formal _____.
- a. Logic0
- b. Thing
- c. Undefined
- d. Undefined

116. _____ Logic is a concept in traditional logic referring to a "type of immediate inference in which from a given proposition another proposition is inferred which has as its subject the predicate of the original proposition and as its predicate the subject of the original proposition (the quality of the proposition being retained)."
- a. Concept
- b. Converse0
- c. Undefined
- d. Undefined

117. In common philosophical language, a proposition or _____, is the content of an assertion, that is, it is true-or-false and defined by the meaning of a particular piece of language.
- a. Concept
- b. Statement0
- c. Undefined
- d. Undefined

118. A _____ of a number is the product of that number with any integer.
- a. Multiple0
- b. Thing
- c. Undefined
- d. Undefined

119. In geometry and trigonometry, a _____ is defined as an angle between two straight intersecting lines of ninety degrees, or one-quarter of a circle.
- a. Right angle0
- b. Thing
- c. Undefined
- d. Undefined

120. _____ is a natural number that has exactly two distinct natural number divisors, which are 1 and the _____ itself.
- a. Thing
- b. Prime number0
- c. Undefined
- d. Undefined

121. In mathematics, a _____ number (or a _____) is a natural number that has exactly two (distinct) natural number divisors, which are 1 and the _____ number itself.
- a. Thing
- b. Prime0
- c. Undefined
- d. Undefined

122. A _____ is a polygon with four sides and four vertices.
- a. Quadrilateral0
- b. Thing
- c. Undefined
- d. Undefined

Chapter 6. Rational Expressions

123. In mathematics, _____ describes an entity with a limit.
   a. Convergent0
   b. Thing
   c. Undefined
   d. Undefined

124. A _____ is a rectangle whose side lengths are in the golden ratio, 1:, that is, approximately 1:1.618.
   a. Golden rectangle0
   b. Thing
   c. Undefined
   d. Undefined

125. In mathematics, the conjugate _____ or adjoint matrix of an m-by-n matrix A with complex entries is the n-by-m matrix A* obtained from A by taking the transpose and then taking the complex conjugate of each entry.
   a. Thing
   b. Pairs0
   c. Undefined
   d. Undefined

126. _____ are the basic objects of study in graph theory. Informally speaking, a graph is a set of objects called points, nodes, or vertices connected by links called lines or edges.
   a. Graphs0
   b. Thing
   c. Undefined
   d. Undefined

127. An _____ is a straight line or curve A to which another curve B approaches closer and closer as one moves along it. As one moves along B, the space between it and the _____ A becomes smaller and smaller, and can in fact be made as small as one could wish by going far enough along. A curve may or may not touch or cross its _____. In fact, the curve may intersect the _____ an infinite number of times.
   a. Asymptote0
   b. Thing
   c. Undefined
   d. Undefined

128. The _____, in practice often shortened to amp, is a unit of electric current, or amount of electric charge per second.
   a. Thing
   b. Amperes0
   c. Undefined
   d. Undefined

129. The _____ of two integers is the smallest positive integer that is a multiple of both intergers.
   a. Least common multiple0
   b. Thing
   c. Undefined
   d. Undefined

130. Two mathematical objects are equal if and only if they are precisely the same in every way. This defines a binary relation, _____, denoted by the sign of _____ "=" in such a way that the statement "x = y" means that x and y are equal.
   a. Equality0
   b. Thing
   c. Undefined
   d. Undefined

131. _____ is a notation for writing numbers that is often used by scientists and mathematicians to make it easier to write large and small numbers.
   a. Scientific notation0
   b. Thing
   c. Undefined
   d. Undefined

Chapter 6. Rational Expressions

132. _____ is the scientific study of celestial objects such as stars, planets, comets, and galaxies; and phenomena that originate outside the Earth's atmosphere.
   a. Astronomy0
   b. Thing
   c. Undefined
   d. Undefined

133. _____ or investing is a term with several closely-related meanings in business management, finance and economics, related to saving or deferring consumption.
   a. Thing
   b. Investment0
   c. Undefined
   d. Undefined

134. _____ is the interdisciplinary scientific study of the atmosphere that focuses on weather processes and forecasting.
   a. Meteorology0
   b. Thing
   c. Undefined
   d. Undefined

135. _____ are activities that are governed by a set of rules or customs and often engaged in competitively.
   a. Sports0
   b. Thing
   c. Undefined
   d. Undefined

Chapter 7. Rational Exponents and Radicals

1. In mathematics, a _____ number is a number which can be expressed as a ratio of two integers. Non-integer _____ numbers (commonly called fractions) are usually written as the vulgar fraction a / b, where b is not zero.
   a. Rational0
   b. Thing
   c. Undefined
   d. Undefined

2. _____ is a mathematical operation, written a^n, involving two numbers, the base a and the exponent n.
   a. Thing
   b. Exponentiating0
   c. Undefined
   d. Undefined

3. _____ is a mathematical operation, written a^n, involving two numbers, the base a and the exponent n.
   a. Thing
   b. Exponentiation0
   c. Undefined
   d. Undefined

4. In mathematics, _____ growth occurs when the growth rate of a function is always proportional to the function's current size.
   a. Exponential0
   b. Thing
   c. Undefined
   d. Undefined

5. An _____ is a combination of numbers, operators, grouping symbols and/or free variables and bound variables arranged in a meaningful way which can be evaluated..
   a. Thing
   b. Expression0
   c. Undefined
   d. Undefined

6. _____ has many meanings, most of which simply .
   a. Power0
   b. Thing
   c. Undefined
   d. Undefined

7. A _____ is a number that is less than zero.
   a. Negative number0
   b. Thing
   c. Undefined
   d. Undefined

8. In mathematics, a _____ may be described informally as a number that can be given by an infinite decimal representation.
   a. Real number0
   b. Thing
   c. Undefined
   d. Undefined

9. Mathematical _____ is used to represent ideas.
   a. Thing
   b. Notation0
   c. Undefined
   d. Undefined

10. _____ is a branch of mathematics concerning the study of structure, relation and quantity.
    a. Algebra0
    b. Concept
    c. Undefined
    d. Undefined

11. In mathematics, _____ expressions is used to reduce the expression into the lowest possible term.

Chapter 7. Rational Exponents and Radicals

a. Thing
b. Simplifying0
c. Undefined
d. Undefined

12. _____ is the symbol used to indicate the nth root of a number
    a. Thing
    b. Radical0
    c. Undefined
    d. Undefined

13. The _____ are the only integral domain whose positive elements are well-ordered, and in which order is preserved by addition. Like the natural numbers, the _____ form a countably infinite set. The set of all _____ is usually denoted in mathematics by a boldface Z .
    a. Thing
    b. Integers0
    c. Undefined
    d. Undefined

14. A _____ is the part of a fraction that tells how many equal parts make up a whole, and which is used in the name of the fraction: "halves", "thirds", "fourths" or "quarters", "fifths" and so on.
    a. Concept
    b. Denominator0
    c. Undefined
    d. Undefined

15. In mathematics, a _____ is the end result of a division problem. It can also be expressed as the number of times the divisor divides into the dividend.
    a. Quotient0
    b. Thing
    c. Undefined
    d. Undefined

16. An _____ of a number a is a number b such that $b^n = a$.
    a. Thing
    b. Nth root0
    c. Undefined
    d. Undefined

17. In mathematics, a _____ of a complex-valued function f is a member x of the domain of f such that f(x) vanishes at x, that is, x : f (x) = 0.
    a. Thing
    b. Root0
    c. Undefined
    d. Undefined

18. _____ was the German mathematician who wrote "Coss," the first german algebra book.
    a. Person
    b. Christoff Rudolff0
    c. Undefined
    d. Undefined

19. The word _____ is used in a variety of ways in mathematics.
    a. Thing
    b. Index0
    c. Undefined
    d. Undefined

20. The _____ is the number or expression underneath the radical sign.
    a. Radicand0
    b. Thing
    c. Undefined
    d. Undefined

21. In plane geometry, a _____ is a polygon with four equal sides, four right angles, and parallel opposite sides. In algebra, the _____ of a number is that number multiplied by itself.

Chapter 7. Rational Exponents and Radicals

    a. Square0
    b. Thing
    c. Undefined
    d. Undefined

22. In mathematics, a _____ of a number x is a number r such that $r^2 = x$, or in words, a number r whose square (the result of multiplying the number by itself) is x.
    a. Square root0
    b. Thing
    c. Undefined
    d. Undefined

23. A _____ is a numeral used to indicate a count. The most common use of the word today is to name the part of a fraction that tells the number or count of equal parts.
    a. Numerator0
    b. Thing
    c. Undefined
    d. Undefined

24. A _____ is a three-dimensional solid object bounded by six square faces, facets, or sides, with three meeting at each vertex.
    a. Thing
    b. Cube0
    c. Undefined
    d. Undefined

25. A _____ of a number is a number a such that $a^3 = x$.
    a. Cube root0
    b. Thing
    c. Undefined
    d. Undefined

26. In mathematics, a _____ is the result of multiplying, or an expression that identifies factors to be multiplied.
    a. Product0
    b. Thing
    c. Undefined
    d. Undefined

27. A _____ is a symbolic representation denoting a quantity or expression. It often represents an "unknown" quantity that has the potential to change.
    a. Variable0
    b. Thing
    c. Undefined
    d. Undefined

28. A _____ is a number which is the cube of an integer.
    a. Perfect cube0
    b. Thing
    c. Undefined
    d. Undefined

29. In mathematics, a _____ of an integer n, also called a factor of n, is an integer which evenly divides n without leaving a remainder.
    a. Divisor0
    b. Thing
    c. Undefined
    d. Undefined

30. In mathematics, factorization (British English: factorisation) or factoring is the decomposition of an object (for example, a number, a polynomial, or a matrix) into a product of other objects, or _____, which when multiplied together give the original.
    a. Thing
    b. Factors0
    c. Undefined
    d. Undefined

Chapter 7. Rational Exponents and Radicals

31. The term _____ can refer to an integer which is the square of some other integer, or an algebraic expression that can be factored as the square of some other expression.
    a. Thing
    b. Perfect square0
    c. Undefined
    d. Undefined

32. In mathematics, an inequality is a statement about the relative size or order of two objects. For example 14 > 10, or 14 is _____ 10.
    a. Thing
    b. Greater than0
    c. Undefined
    d. Undefined

33. In mathematics, _____ are used to indicate the square root of a number.
    a. Radicals0
    b. Thing
    c. Undefined
    d. Undefined

34. The _____, the average in everyday English, which is also called the arithmetic _____ (and is distinguished from the geometric _____ or harmonic _____). The average is also called the sample _____. The expected value of a random variable, which is also called the population _____.
    a. Mean0
    b. Thing
    c. Undefined
    d. Undefined

35. _____ is the fee paid on borrowed money.
    a. Thing
    b. Interest0
    c. Undefined
    d. Undefined

36. In mathematics, an _____ number is any real number that is not a rational number- that is, it is a number which cannot be expressed as a fraction m/n, where m and n are integers.
    a. Thing
    b. Irrational0
    c. Undefined
    d. Undefined

37. In mathematics, an _____ is any real number that is not a rational number ¡ª that is, it is a number which cannot be expressed as m/n, where m and n are integers.
    a. Thing
    b. Irrational number0
    c. Undefined
    d. Undefined

38. In mathematics, _____ are any real number that is not a rational number ¡ª that is, it is a number which cannot be expressed as m/n, where m and n are integers.
    a. Thing
    b. Irrational numbers0
    c. Undefined
    d. Undefined

39. Julius Wilhelm Richard _____ (October 6, 1831 – February 12, 1916) was a German mathematician who did important work in abstract algebra, algebraic number theory and the foundations of the real numbers.
    a. Dedekind0
    b. Person
    c. Undefined
    d. Undefined

40. _____ is the state of being greater than any finite real or natural number, however large.

Chapter 7. Rational Exponents and Radicals

a. Thing
b. Infinite0
c. Undefined
d. Undefined

41. _____ is the state of being greater than any finite number, however large.
a. Thing
b. Infinity0
c. Undefined
d. Undefined

42. A _____ is the result of the addition of a set of numbers. The numbers may be natural numbers, complex numbers, matrices, or still more complicated objects. An infinite _____ is a subtle procedure known as a series.
a. Sum0
b. Thing
c. Undefined
d. Undefined

43. In mathematics, and in particular in abstract algebra, the _____ is a property of binary operations that generalises the distributive law from elementary algebra.
a. Thing
b. Distributive property0
c. Undefined
d. Undefined

44. _____, either of the curved-bracket punctuation marks that together make a set of _____
a. Parentheses0
b. Thing
c. Undefined
d. Undefined

45. _____ also sometimes known as the double distributive property or more colloquially as foiling, is commonly taught to US high school students learning algebra as a mnemonic for remembering how to multiply two binomials polynomials with two terms.
a. FOIL method0
b. Thing
c. Undefined
d. Undefined

46. The _____ is commonly taught to US high school students learning algebra as a mnemonic for remembering how to multiply two binomials.
a. FOIL rule0
b. Thing
c. Undefined
d. Undefined

47. In algebra, a _____ is a binomial formed by taking the opposite of the second term of a binomial.
a. Thing
b. Conjugate0
c. Undefined
d. Undefined

48. _____, or Rationalisation in mathematics is the process of removing a square root or imaginary number from the denominator of a fraction.
a. Thing
b. Rationalizing0
c. Undefined
d. Undefined

49. In mathematics, the additive inverse, or _____ of a number n is the number that, when added to n, yields zero. The additive inverse of n is denoted −n. For example, 7 is −7, because 7 + (−7) = 0, and the additive inverse of −0.3 is 0.3, because −0.3 + 0.3 = 0.

a. Thing
b. Opposite0
c. Undefined
d. Undefined

50. In mathematics, the _____ of a number n is the number that, when added to n, yields zero. The _____ of n is denoted −n. For example, 7 is −7, because 7 + (−7) = 0, and the _____ of −0.3 is 0.3, because −0.3 + 0.3 = 0.
a. Thing
b. Additive inverse0
c. Undefined
d. Undefined

51. The mathematical concept of a _____ expresses the intuitive idea of deterministic dependence between two quantities, one of which is viewed as primary and the other as secondary. A _____ then is a way to associate a unique output for each input of a specified type, for example, a real number or an element of a given set.
a. Function0
b. Thing
c. Undefined
d. Undefined

52. In mathematics, a _____ of a k-place relation $L \subseteq X_1 \times ... \times X_k$ is one of the sets X_j, $1 \leq j \leq k$. In the special case where k = 2 and $L \subseteq X_1 \times X_2$ is a function $L : X_1 \rightarrow X_2$, it is conventional to refer to X_1 as the _____ of the function and to refer to X_2 as the codomain of the function.
a. Domain0
b. Thing
c. Undefined
d. Undefined

53. In mathematics, an _____ is a statement about the relative size or order of two objects.
a. Inequality0
b. Thing
c. Undefined
d. Undefined

54. In elementary algebra, an _____ is a set that contains every real number between two indicated numbers and may contain the two numbers themselves.
a. Interval0
b. Thing
c. Undefined
d. Undefined

55. _____ is the notation in which permitted values for a variable are expressed as ranging over a certain interval; "5 < x < 9" is an example of the application of _____.
a. Interval notation0
b. Thing
c. Undefined
d. Undefined

56. _____ the expected value of a random variable displays the average or central value of the variable. It is a summary value of the distribution of the variable.
a. Thing
b. Determining0
c. Undefined
d. Undefined

57. An _____ is a collection of two not necessarily distinct objects, one of which is distinguished as the first coordinate and the other as the second coordinate.
a. Ordered pair0
b. Thing
c. Undefined
d. Undefined

58. In mathematics, the conjugate _____ or adjoint matrix of an m-by-n matrix A with complex entries is the n-by-m matrix A* obtained from A by taking the transpose and then taking the complex conjugate of each entry.

Chapter 7. Rational Exponents and Radicals 97

    a. Thing
    c. Undefined
    b. Pairs0
    d. Undefined

59. _____ is a synonym for information.
    a. Thing
    c. Undefined
    b. Data0
    d. Undefined

60. In mathematics, an _____, mean, or central tendency of a data set refers to a measure of the "middle" or "expected" value of the data set.
    a. Average0
    c. Undefined
    b. Concept
    d. Undefined

61. _____ are the basic objects of study in graph theory. Informally speaking, a graph is a set of objects called points, nodes, or vertices connected by links called lines or edges.
    a. Thing
    c. Undefined
    b. Graphs0
    d. Undefined

62. In common philosophical language, a proposition or _____, is the content of an assertion, that is, it is true-or-false and defined by the meaning of a particular piece of language.
    a. Statement0
    c. Undefined
    b. Concept
    d. Undefined

63. The deductive-nomological model is a formalized view of scientific _____ in natural language.
    a. Thing
    c. Undefined
    b. Explanation0
    d. Undefined

64. _____ Logic is a concept in traditional logic referring to a "type of immediate inference in which from a given proposition another proposition is inferred which has as its subject the predicate of the original proposition and as its predicate the subject of the original proposition (the quality of the proposition being retained)."
    a. Converse0
    c. Undefined
    b. Concept
    d. Undefined

65. A _____ is a negotiable instrument instructing a financial institution to pay a specific amount of a specific currency from a specific demand account held in the maker/depositor's name with that institution. Both the maker and payee may be natural persons or legal entities.
    a. Thing
    c. Undefined
    b. Check0
    d. Undefined

66. _____ variables are variables other than the independent variable that may bear any effect on the behavior of the subject being studied.
    a. Thing
    c. Undefined
    b. Extraneous0
    d. Undefined

67. In physics, a _____ may refer to the scalar _____ or to the vector _____.

Chapter 7. Rational Exponents and Radicals

    a. Thing
    b. Potential0
    c. Undefined
    d. Undefined

68. In mathematics, a _____ is a polynomial equation of the second degree. The general form is $ax^2 + bx + c = 0$.
    a. Thing
    b. Quadratic equation0
    c. Undefined
    d. Undefined

69. _____ is a notation for writing numbers that is often used by scientists and mathematicians to make it easier to write large and small numbers.
    a. Thing
    b. Scientific notation0
    c. Undefined
    d. Undefined

70. The _____ of a right triangle is the triangle's longest side; the side opposite the right angle.
    a. Hypotenuse0
    b. Thing
    c. Undefined
    d. Undefined

71. A _____ is one of the basic shapes of geometry: a polygon with three vertices and three sides which are straight line segments.
    a. Triangle0
    b. Thing
    c. Undefined
    d. Undefined

72. _____ was an Greek philosopher. He is best known for a theorem in trigonometry that bears his name.
    a. Person
    b. Pythagoras0
    c. Undefined
    d. Undefined

73. In a right triangle, the _____ of the triangle are the two sides that are perpendicular to each other, as opposed to the hypotenuse.
    a. Legs0
    b. Thing
    c. Undefined
    d. Undefined

74. _____ has one 90° internal angle a right angle.
    a. Right triangle0
    b. Thing
    c. Undefined
    d. Undefined

75. _____ is a relation in Euclidean geometry among the three sides of a right triangle.
    a. Pythagorean Theorem0
    b. Thing
    c. Undefined
    d. Undefined

76. In mathematics, a _____ is a statement that can be proved on the basis of explicitly stated or previously agreed assumptions.
    a. Theorem0
    b. Thing
    c. Undefined
    d. Undefined

77. In geometry, a _____ is defined as a quadrilateral where all four of its angles are right angles.

Chapter 7. Rational Exponents and Radicals

  a. Rectangle0
  b. Thing
  c. Undefined
  d. Undefined

78. A _____ can refer to a line joining two nonadjacent vertices of a polygon or polyhedron, or in some contexts any upward or downward sloping line. .
  a. Thing
  b. Diagonal0
  c. Undefined
  d. Undefined

79. _____ is the scientific study of celestial objects such as stars, planets, comets, and galaxies; and phenomena that originate outside the Earth's atmosphere.
  a. Astronomy0
  b. Thing
  c. Undefined
  d. Undefined

80. A _____, as defined by the International Astronomical Union , is a celestial body orbiting a star or stellar remnant that is massive enough to be rounded by its own gravity, not massive enough to cause thermonuclear fusion in its core, and has cleared its neighboring region of planetesimals.
  a. Planet0
  b. Thing
  c. Undefined
  d. Undefined

81. A _____ is a unit of length, usually used to measure distance, in a number of different systems, including Imperial units, United States customary units and Norwegian/Swedish mil. Its size can vary from system to system, but in each is between 1 and 10 kilometers. In contemporary English contexts _____ refers to either:
  a. Thing
  b. Mile0
  c. Undefined
  d. Undefined

82. The _____ of measurement are a globally standardized and modernized form of the metric system.
  a. Units0
  b. Thing
  c. Undefined
  d. Undefined

83. _____ of an object is its speed in a particular direction.
  a. Velocity0
  b. Thing
  c. Undefined
  d. Undefined

84. Compass and straightedge or ruler-and-compass _____ is the _____ of lengths or angles using only an idealized ruler and compass.
  a. Thing
  b. Construction0
  c. Undefined
  d. Undefined

85. A _____ is a special kind of ratio, indicating a relationship between two measurements with different units, such as miles to gallons or cents to pounds.
  a. Rate0
  b. Thing
  c. Undefined
  d. Undefined

86. _____ is the level of functional and/or metabolic efficiency of an organism at both the micro level.

Chapter 7. Rational Exponents and Radicals

a. Thing
b. Health0
c. Undefined
d. Undefined

87. _____ is the transport of people on a trip/journey or the process or time involved in a person or object moving from one location to another.
a. Thing
b. Travel0
c. Undefined
d. Undefined

88. In geometry, a _____ is a special kind of point, usually a corner of a polygon, polyhedron, or higher dimensional polytope. In the geometry of curves a _____ is a point of where the first derivative of curvature is zero. In graph theory, a _____ is the fundamental unit out of which graphs are formed
a. Thing
b. Vertex0
c. Undefined
d. Undefined

89. _____, Greek for "knowledge of nature," is the branch of science concerned with the discovery and characterization of universal laws which govern matter, energy, space, and time.
a. Physics0
b. Thing
c. Undefined
d. Undefined

90. _____ is defined as the rate of change or derivative with respect to time of velocity.
a. Thing
b. Acceleration0
c. Undefined
d. Undefined

91. In mathematics, the _____ of a complex number z, is the first element of the ordered pair of real numbers representing z, i.e. if z = (x,y), or equivalently, z = x + iy, then the _____ of z is x. It is denoted by Re{z} . The complex function which maps z to the _____ of z is not holomorphic.
a. Thing
b. Real part0
c. Undefined
d. Undefined

92. In mathematics, an _____ number is a complex number whose square is a negative real number. They were defined in 1572 by Rafael Bombelli.
a. Thing
b. Imaginary0
c. Undefined
d. Undefined

93. In mathematics, a _____ is a number in the form of a + bi where a and b are real numbers, and i is the imaginary unit, with the property i 2 = −1. The real number a is called the real part of the _____, and the real number b is the imaginary part.
a. Complex number0
b. Thing
c. Undefined
d. Undefined

94. In mathematics, the _____ of a complex number z, is the second element of the ordered pair of real numbers representing z, i.e. if z = (x,y), or equivalently, z = x + iy, then the _____ of z is y.
a. Imaginary part0
b. Thing
c. Undefined
d. Undefined

95. A _____ of a number is the product of that number with any integer.

Chapter 7. Rational Exponents and Radicals

a. Thing
b. Multiple0
c. Undefined
d. Undefined

96. _____ forms part of thinking. Considered the most complex of all intellectual functions, _____ has been defined as higher-order cognitive process that requires the modulation and control of more routine or fundamental skills.
a. Thing
b. Problem solving0
c. Undefined
d. Undefined

97. In mathematics, _____ is the decomposition of an object into a product of other objects, or factors, which when multiplied together give the original.
a. Factoring0
b. Thing
c. Undefined
d. Undefined

98. _____, in number theory is the process of breaking down a composite number into smaller non-trivial divisors, which when multiplied together equal the original integer.
a. Integer factorization0
b. Thing
c. Undefined
d. Undefined

99. In mathematics, a _____ number (or a _____) is a natural number that has exactly two (distinct) natural number divisors, which are 1 and the _____ number itself.
a. Prime0
b. Thing
c. Undefined
d. Undefined

100. An _____ is a straight line around which a geometric figure can be rotated.
a. Thing
b. Axis0
c. Undefined
d. Undefined

101. In astronomy, geography, geometry and related sciences and contexts, a plane is said to be _____ at a given point if it is locally perpendicular to the gradient of the gravity field, i.e., with the direction of the gravitational force at that point.
a. Horizontal0
b. Thing
c. Undefined
d. Undefined

102. A _____ is a simplified and structured visual representation of concepts, ideas, constructions, relations, statistical data, anatomy etc used in all aspects of human activities to visualize and clarify the topic.
a. Thing
b. Diagram0
c. Undefined
d. Undefined

103. In mathematics, a _____ is a two-dimensional manifold or surface that is perfectly flat.
a. Thing
b. Plane0
c. Undefined
d. Undefined

104. In mathematics, _____ is an elementary arithmetic operation. When one of the numbers is a whole number, _____ is the repeated sum of the other number.
a. Multiplication0
b. Thing
c. Undefined
d. Undefined

Chapter 7. Rational Exponents and Radicals

105. In mathematics, a _____ is an n-tuple with n being 3.
 a. Thing
 b. Triple0
 c. Undefined
 d. Undefined

106. The _____ of a mathematical object is its size: a property by which it can be larger or smaller than other objects of the same kind; in technical terms, an ordering of the class of objects to which it belongs.
 a. Thing
 b. Magnitude0
 c. Undefined
 d. Undefined

107. _____ is often used to describe the measurement of the steepness, incline, gradient, or grade of a straight line. The _____ is defined as the ratio of the "rise" divided by the "run" between two points on a line, or in other words, the ratio of the altitude change to the horizontal distance between any two points on the line.
 a. Thing
 b. Slope0
 c. Undefined
 d. Undefined

108. In mathematics, the _____ of a coordinate system is the point where the axes of the system intersect.
 a. Thing
 b. Origin0
 c. Undefined
 d. Undefined

109. In a mathematical proof or a syllogism, a _____ is a statement that is the logical consequence of preceding statements.
 a. Concept
 b. Conclusion0
 c. Undefined
 d. Undefined

110. A _____ is a set of numbers that designate location in a given reference system, such as x,y in a planar _____ system or an x,y,z in a three-dimensional _____ system.
 a. Thing
 b. Coordinate0
 c. Undefined
 d. Undefined

111. A _____ is a set of possible values that a variable can take on in order to satisfy a given set of conditions, which may include equations and inequalities.
 a. Solution set0
 b. Thing
 c. Undefined
 d. Undefined

112. In mathematics, the concept of a _____ tries to capture the intuitive idea of a geometrical one-dimensional and continuous object. A simple example is the circle.
 a. Curve0
 b. Thing
 c. Undefined
 d. Undefined

113. In mathematics, there are several meanings of _____ depending on the subject.
 a. Thing
 b. Degree0
 c. Undefined
 d. Undefined

114. A _____ is a rectangle whose side lengths are in the golden ratio, 1:, that is, approximately 1:1.618.

Chapter 7. Rational Exponents and Radicals

a. Golden rectangle0
b. Thing
c. Undefined
d. Undefined

115. A _____ is a quantity that denotes the proportional amount or magnitude of one quantity relative to another.
  a. Ratio0
  b. Thing
  c. Undefined
  d. Undefined

116. _____ is the art and science of designing buildings and structures.
  a. Thing
  b. Architecture0
  c. Undefined
  d. Undefined

117. _____ is a kind of property which exists as magnitude or multitude. It is among the basic classes of things along with quality, substance, change, and relation.
  a. Thing
  b. Amount0
  c. Undefined
  d. Undefined

118. _____ is a unit of speed, expressing the number of international miles covered per hour.
  a. Thing
  b. Miles per hour0
  c. Undefined
  d. Undefined

119. In algebra, a _____ is a function depending on n that associates a scalar, $det(A)$, to every $n \times n$ square matrix A.
  a. Thing
  b. Determinant0
  c. Undefined
  d. Undefined

120. _____ or investing is a term with several closely-related meanings in business management, finance and economics, related to saving or deferring consumption.
  a. Thing
  b. Investment0
  c. Undefined
  d. Undefined

121. _____, from Latin meaning "to make progress", is defined in two different ways. Pure economic _____ is the increase in wealth that an investor has from making an investment, taking into consideration all costs associated with that investment including the opportunity cost of capital.
  a. Thing
  b. Profit0
  c. Undefined
  d. Undefined

122. _____ is a business term for the amount of money that a company receives from its activities in a given period, mostly from sales of products and/or services to customers
  a. Thing
  b. Revenue0
  c. Undefined
  d. Undefined

123. Deductive _____ is the kind of _____ in which the conclusion is necessitated by, or reached from, previously known facts (the premises).
  a. Reasoning0
  b. Thing
  c. Undefined
  d. Undefined

Chapter 7. Rational Exponents and Radicals

124. _____ is a term used in accounting, economics and finance with reference to the fact that assets with finite lives lose value over time.
   a. Thing
   b. Depreciation0
   c. Undefined
   d. Undefined

125. In mathematics, for a statement to be mathematically _____, such a statement must be true of all natural numbers.
   a. Inductive0
   b. Thing
   c. Undefined
   d. Undefined

126. Induction or _____, sometimes called inductive logic, is the process of reasoning in which the premises of an argument are believed to support the conclusion but do not ensure it.
   a. Inductive reasoning0
   b. Thing
   c. Undefined
   d. Undefined

127. _____ is the application of tools and a processing medium to the transformation of raw materials into finished goods for sale.
   a. Thing
   b. Manufacturing0
   c. Undefined
   d. Undefined

128. _____ is the design, analysis, and/or construction of works for practical purposes.
   a. Thing
   b. Engineering0
   c. Undefined
   d. Undefined

129. _____ primarily refers to social welfare service concerned with social protection, or protection against socially recognized conditions, including poverty, old age, disability, unemployment, families with children and others.
   a. Thing
   b. Social security0
   c. Undefined
   d. Undefined

130. _____ are activities that are governed by a set of rules or customs and often engaged in competitively.
   a. Sports0
   b. Thing
   c. Undefined
   d. Undefined

131. Transport or _____ is the movement of people and goods from one place to another.
   a. Thing
   b. Transportation0
   c. Undefined
   d. Undefined

Chapter 8. Quadratic Equations and Inequalities

1. In mathematics, a _____ is a polynomial equation of the second degree. The general form is $ax^2 + bx + c = 0$.
   a. Thing
   b. Quadratic equation0
   c. Undefined
   d. Undefined

2. In plane geometry, a _____ is a polygon with four equal sides, four right angles, and parallel opposite sides. In algebra, the _____ of a number is that number multiplied by itself.
   a. Thing
   b. Square0
   c. Undefined
   d. Undefined

3. In mathematics, a _____ of a number x is a number r such that $r^2 = x$, or in words, a number r whose square (the result of multiplying the number by itself) is x.
   a. Square root0
   b. Thing
   c. Undefined
   d. Undefined

4. In mathematics, a _____ is a constant multiplicative factor of a certain object. The object can be such things as a variable, a vector, a function, etc. For example, the _____ of $9x^2$ is 9.
   a. Thing
   b. Coefficient0
   c. Undefined
   d. Undefined

5. In mathematics, _____ is the decomposition of an object into a product of other objects, or factors, which when multiplied together give the original.
   a. Factoring0
   b. Thing
   c. Undefined
   d. Undefined

6. In mathematics, a _____ of a complex-valued function f is a member x of the domain of f such that f(x) vanishes at x, that is, x : f (x) = 0.
   a. Root0
   b. Thing
   c. Undefined
   d. Undefined

7. _____ is a notation for writing numbers that is often used by scientists and mathematicians to make it easier to write large and small numbers.
   a. Scientific notation0
   b. Thing
   c. Undefined
   d. Undefined

8. In mathematics, a _____ is an expression that is constructed from one or more variables and constants, using only the operations of addition, subtraction, multiplication, and constant positive whole number exponents. is a _____. Note in particular that division by an expression containing a variable is not in general allowed in polynomials. [1]
   a. Polynomial0
   b. Thing
   c. Undefined
   d. Undefined

9. In mathematics and the mathematical sciences, a _____ is a fixed, but possibly unspecified, value. This is in contrast to a variable, which is not fixed.
   a. Thing
   b. Constant0
   c. Undefined
   d. Undefined

10. In mathematics, there are several meanings of _____ depending on the subject.

a. Thing
b. Degree0
c. Undefined
d. Undefined

11. In mathematics, a _____ is the result of multiplying, or an expression that identifies factors to be multiplied.
    a. Product0
    b. Thing
    c. Undefined
    d. Undefined

12. In mathematics, factorization (British English: factorisation) or factoring is the decomposition of an object (for example, a number, a polynomial, or a matrix) into a product of other objects, or _____, which when multiplied together give the original.
    a. Factors0
    b. Thing
    c. Undefined
    d. Undefined

13. A _____ signifies a point or points of probability on a subject e.g., the _____ of creativity, which allows for the formation of rule or norm or law by interpretation of the phenomena events that can be created.
    a. Thing
    b. Principle0
    c. Undefined
    d. Undefined

14. A _____ is a negotiable instrument instructing a financial institution to pay a specific amount of a specific currency from a specific demand account held in the maker/depositor's name with that institution. Both the maker and payee may be natural persons or legal entities.
    a. Check0
    b. Thing
    c. Undefined
    d. Undefined

15. The _____, the average in everyday English, which is also called the arithmetic _____ (and is distinguished from the geometric _____ or harmonic _____). The average is also called the sample _____. The expected value of a random variable, which is also called the population _____.
    a. Thing
    b. Mean0
    c. Undefined
    d. Undefined

16. In mathematics, a _____ is a number in the form of a + bi where a and b are real numbers, and i is the imaginary unit, with the property $i^2 = -1$. The real number a is called the real part of the _____, and the real number b is the imaginary part.
    a. Complex number0
    b. Thing
    c. Undefined
    d. Undefined

17. A _____ is the part of a fraction that tells how many equal parts make up a whole, and which is used in the name of the fraction: "halves", "thirds", "fourths" or "quarters", "fifths" and so on.
    a. Denominator0
    b. Concept
    c. Undefined
    d. Undefined

18. In elementary algebra, a _____ is a polynomial with two terms: the sum of two monomials. It is the simplest kind of polynomial except for a monomial.
    a. Thing
    b. Binomial0
    c. Undefined
    d. Undefined

Chapter 8. Quadratic Equations and Inequalities

19. A _____ is a quantity that denotes the proportional amount or magnitude of one quantity relative to another.
   a. Ratio0
   b. Thing
   c. Undefined
   d. Undefined

20. In chemistry, a _____ is substance made by combining two or more different materials in such a way that no chemical reaction occurs.
   a. Thing
   b. Mixture0
   c. Undefined
   d. Undefined

21. In mathematics, a _____ may be described informally as a number that can be given by an infinite decimal representation.
   a. Real number0
   b. Thing
   c. Undefined
   d. Undefined

22. In algebra, a _____ is a binomial formed by taking the opposite of the second term of a binomial.
   a. Conjugate0
   b. Thing
   c. Undefined
   d. Undefined

23. The system of _____ numerals was a numeral system used in ancient Egypt. It was a decimal system, often rounded off to the higher power, written in hieroglyphs.
   a. Thing
   b. Egyptian0
   c. Undefined
   d. Undefined

24. A _____ was a citizen of Babylonia, named for its capital city, Babylon, which was an ancient state in the south part of Mesopotamia (in modern Iraq), combining the territories of Sumer and Akkad.
   a. Place
   b. Babylonian0
   c. Undefined
   d. Undefined

25. A quadratic equation with real solutions, called roots, which may be real or complex, is given by the _____: $x = \frac{-b \pm \sqrt{b^2 - 4ac}}{2a}$.
   a. Thing
   b. Quadratic formula0
   c. Undefined
   d. Undefined

26. _____ is a technique used in algebra to solve quadratic equations, in analytic geometry for determining the shapes of graphs, and in calculus for computing integrals, including, but hardly limited to, the integrals that define Laplace transforms. The essential objective is to reduce a quadratic polynomial in a variable in an equation or expression to a squared polynomial of linear order. This can reduce an equation or integral to one that is more easily solved or evaluated.
   a. Thing
   b. Completing the square0
   c. Undefined
   d. Undefined

27. A _____ is a polynomial consisting of three terms; in other words, it is the sum of three monomials.
   a. Thing
   b. Trinomial0
   c. Undefined
   d. Undefined

28. _____ is a fixed, but possibly unspecified, value. This is in contrast to a variable, which is not fixed.

a. Constant term0 b. Thing
c. Undefined d. Undefined

29. _____ is the fee paid on borrowed money.
   a. Interest0 b. Thing
   c. Undefined d. Undefined

30. _____ is the process of reducing the number of significant digits in a number.
   a. Rounding0 b. Concept
   c. Undefined d. Undefined

31. Initial objects are also called _____, and terminal objects are also called final.
   a. Thing b. Coterminal0
   c. Undefined d. Undefined

32. In Euclidean geometry, a _____ is the set of all points in a plane at a fixed distance, called the radius, from a given point, the center.
   a. Circle0 b. Thing
   c. Undefined d. Undefined

33. A _____ is a tool similar to a ruler, but without markings.
   a. Thing b. Straightedge0
   c. Undefined d. Undefined

34. Compass and straightedge or ruler-and-compass _____ is the _____ of lengths or angles using only an idealized ruler and compass.
   a. Thing b. Construction0
   c. Undefined d. Undefined

35. The term _____ can refer to an integer which is the square of some other integer, or an algebraic expression that can be factored as the square of some other expression.
   a. Thing b. Perfect square0
   c. Undefined d. Undefined

36. In mathematics, a _____ number is a number which can be expressed as a ratio of two integers. Non-integer _____ numbers (commonly called fractions) are usually written as the vulgar fraction a / b, where b is not zero.
   a. Thing b. Rational0
   c. Undefined d. Undefined

37. _____ of a polynomial with real or complex coefficients is a certain expression in the coefficients of the polynomial which is equal to zero if and only if the polynomial has a multiple root i.e. a root with multiplicity greater than one in the complex numbers.
   a. Discriminant0 b. Thing
   c. Undefined d. Undefined

Chapter 8. Quadratic Equations and Inequalities

38. In mathematics, an inequality is a statement about the relative size or order of two objects. For example 14 > 10, or 14 is _____ 10.
    a. Thing
    b. Greater than0
    c. Undefined
    d. Undefined

39. An _____ is a combination of numbers, operators, grouping symbols and/or free variables and bound variables arranged in a meaningful way which can be evaluated..
    a. Thing
    b. Expression0
    c. Undefined
    d. Undefined

40. In mathematics, an _____ number is any real number that is not a rational number- that is, it is a number which cannot be expressed as a fraction m/n, where m and n are integers.
    a. Thing
    b. Irrational0
    c. Undefined
    d. Undefined

41. _____ is the symbold used to indicate the nth root of a number
    a. Radical0
    b. Thing
    c. Undefined
    d. Undefined

42. The word _____ comes from the Latin word linearis, which means created by lines.
    a. Thing
    b. Linear0
    c. Undefined
    d. Undefined

43. _____ are activities that are governed by a set of rules or customs and often engaged in competitively.
    a. Thing
    b. Sports0
    c. Undefined
    d. Undefined

44. In logic and mathematics, logical _____ (usual symbol and) is a two-place logical operation that results in a value of true if both of its operands are true, otherwise a value of false.
    a. Concept
    b. Conjunction0
    c. Undefined
    d. Undefined

45. In sociology and biology a _____ is the collection of people or organisms of a particular species living in a given geographic area or space, usually measured by a census.
    a. Population0
    b. Thing
    c. Undefined
    d. Undefined

46. _____ primarily refers to social welfare service concerned with social protection, or protection against socially recognized conditions, including poverty, old age, disability, unemployment, families with children and others.
    a. Social security0
    b. Thing
    c. Undefined
    d. Undefined

47. In mathematics, a _____ is a homogeneous polynomial of degree two in a number of variables.
    a. Thing
    b. Quadratic form0
    c. Undefined
    d. Undefined

Chapter 8. Quadratic Equations and Inequalities

48. A _____ is a symbolic representation denoting a quantity or expression. It often represents an "unknown" quantity that has the potential to change.
 a. Thing
 b. Variable0
 c. Undefined
 d. Undefined

49. _____ variables are variables other than the independent variable that may bear any effect on the behavior of the subject being studied.
 a. Thing
 b. Extraneous0
 c. Undefined
 d. Undefined

50. In geometry, the _____ of an object is a point in some sense in the middle of the object.
 a. Thing
 b. Center0
 c. Undefined
 d. Undefined

51. In geometry, a _____ is the intersection of a body in 2-dimensional space with a line, or of a body in 3-dimensional space with a plane
 a. Cross section0
 b. Thing
 c. Undefined
 d. Undefined

52. In classical geometry, a _____ of a circle or sphere is any line segment from its center to its boundary. By extension, the _____ of a circle or sphere is the length of any such segment. The _____ is half the diameter. In science and engineering the term _____ of curvature is commonly used as a synonym for _____.
 a. Radius0
 b. Thing
 c. Undefined
 d. Undefined

53. A _____ is a set of numbers that designate location in a given reference system, such as x,y in a planar _____ system or an x,y,z in a three-dimensional _____ system.
 a. Coordinate0
 b. Thing
 c. Undefined
 d. Undefined

54. An _____ is when two lines intersect somewhere on a plane creating a right angle at intersection
 a. Axes0
 b. Thing
 c. Undefined
 d. Undefined

55. In mathematics and more specifically set theory, the _____ set is the unique set which contains no elements.
 a. Thing
 b. Empty0
 c. Undefined
 d. Undefined

56. A _____ is a special kind of ratio, indicating a relationship between two measurements with different units, such as miles to gallons or cents to pounds.
 a. Thing
 b. Rate0
 c. Undefined
 d. Undefined

57. A _____ is a number that is less than zero.

Chapter 8. Quadratic Equations and Inequalities

 a. Thing   b. Negative number0
 c. Undefined   d. Undefined

58. A _____ is the result of the addition of a set of numbers. The numbers may be natural numbers, complex numbers, matrices, or still more complicated objects. An infinite _____ is a subtle procedure known as a series.
 a. Thing   b. Sum0
 c. Undefined   d. Undefined

59. In geometry, a _____ is defined as a quadrilateral where all four of its angles are right angles.
 a. Thing   b. Rectangle0
 c. Undefined   d. Undefined

60. _____ is a kind of property which exists as magnitude or multitude. It is among the basic classes of things along with quality, substance, change, and relation.
 a. Amount0   b. Thing
 c. Undefined   d. Undefined

61. The _____ of a right circular cone is the distance from any point on the circle to the apex of the cone.
 a. Slant height0   b. Thing
 c. Undefined   d. Undefined

62. _____ is the application of tools and a processing medium to the transformation of raw materials into finished goods for sale.
 a. Thing   b. Manufacturing0
 c. Undefined   d. Undefined

63. A _____ is a three-dimensional geometric shape formed by straight lines through a fixed point (vertex) to the points of a fixed curve (directrix)
 a. Cone0   b. Concept
 c. Undefined   d. Undefined

64. The State of _____ is a state located in the Rocky Mountain region of the United States of America.
 a. Thing   b. Colorado0
 c. Undefined   d. Undefined

65. Transport or _____ is the movement of people and goods from one place to another.
 a. Transportation0   b. Thing
 c. Undefined   d. Undefined

66. In mathematics, an _____, mean, or central tendency of a data set refers to a measure of the "middle" or "expected" value of the data set.
 a. Average0   b. Concept
 c. Undefined   d. Undefined

67. A _____ is any object propelled through space by the applicationp of a force.

112 *Chapter 8. Quadratic Equations and Inequalities*

    a. Projectile0   b. Thing
    c. Undefined   d. Undefined

68. _____ of an object is its speed in a particular direction.
    a. Thing   b. Velocity0
    c. Undefined   d. Undefined

69. _____, Greek for "knowledge of nature," is the branch of science concerned with the discovery and characterization of universal laws which govern matter, energy, space, and time.
    a. Thing   b. Physics0
    c. Undefined   d. Undefined

70. A _____ is a unit of length in the metric system, equal to one thousand metres, the current SI base unit of length
    a. Thing   b. Kilometer0
    c. Undefined   d. Undefined

71. The metre (or _____, see spelling differences) is a measure of length. It is the basic unit of length in the metric system and in the International System of Units (SI), used around the world for general and scientific purposes.
    a. Concept   b. Meter0
    c. Undefined   d. Undefined

72. A _____ is a vehicle, missile or aircraft which obtains thrust by the reaction to the ejection of fast moving fluid from within a _____ engine.
    a. Rocket0   b. Thing
    c. Undefined   d. Undefined

73. _____ is the design, analysis, and/or construction of works for practical purposes.
    a. Engineering0   b. Thing
    c. Undefined   d. Undefined

74. The _____ of measurement are a globally standardized and modernized form of the metric system.
    a. Units0   b. Thing
    c. Undefined   d. Undefined

75. In mathematics, a _____ is a two-dimensional manifold or surface that is perfectly flat.
    a. Plane0   b. Thing
    c. Undefined   d. Undefined

76. _____ is the transport of people on a trip/journey or the process or time involved in a person or object moving from one location to another.
    a. Travel0   b. Thing
    c. Undefined   d. Undefined

77. A _____ is a numeral used to indicate a count. The most common use of the word today is to name the part of a fraction that tells the number or count of equal parts.

Chapter 8. Quadratic Equations and Inequalities

   a. Numerator0
   b. Thing
   c. Undefined
   d. Undefined

78. In mathematics, the multiplicative inverse of a number x, denoted 1/x or x^{-1}, is the number which, when multiplied by x, yields 1. The multiplicative inverse of x is also called the _____ of x.
   a. Thing
   b. Reciprocal0
   c. Undefined
   d. Undefined

79. A _____ is a three-dimensional solid object bounded by six square faces, facets, or sides, with three meeting at each vertex.
   a. Thing
   b. Cube0
   c. Undefined
   d. Undefined

80. _____ are of a number n in its third power-the result of multiplying it by itself three times.
   a. Cubes0
   b. Thing
   c. Undefined
   d. Undefined

81. The _____ are the only integral domain whose positive elements are well-ordered, and in which order is preserved by addition. Like the natural numbers, the _____ form a countably infinite set. The set of all _____ is usually denoted in mathematics by a boldface Z .
   a. Integers0
   b. Thing
   c. Undefined
   d. Undefined

82. _____ means in succession or back-to-back
   a. Consecutive0
   b. Thing
   c. Undefined
   d. Undefined

83. In mathematics, a _____ is the set of all points in three-dimensional space (R^3) which are at distance r from a fixed point of that space, where r is a positive real number called the radius of the _____. The fixed point is called the center or centre, and is not part of the _____ itself.
   a. Sphere0
   b. Thing
   c. Undefined
   d. Undefined

84. In mathematics, an _____ is a statement about the relative size or order of two objects.
   a. Thing
   b. Inequality0
   c. Undefined
   d. Undefined

85. A _____ is a set of possible values that a variable can take on in order to satisfy a given set of conditions, which may include equations and inequalities.
   a. Solution set0
   b. Thing
   c. Undefined
   d. Undefined

86. A _____ is a one-dimensional picture in which the integers are shown as specially-marked points evenly spaced on a line.

114 Chapter 8. Quadratic Equations and Inequalities

a. Number line0
b. Thing
c. Undefined
d. Undefined

87. _____ systems represent systems whose behavior is not expressible as a sum of the behaviors of its descriptors.
   a. Nonlinear0
   b. Thing
   c. Undefined
   d. Undefined

88. In abstract algebra, _____ consists of sets with binary operations that satisfy certain axioms.
   a. Grouping0
   b. Thing
   c. Undefined
   d. Undefined

89. In mathematics, a _____ is the end result of a division problem. It can also be expressed as the number of times the divisor divides into the dividend.
   a. Thing
   b. Quotient0
   c. Undefined
   d. Undefined

90. _____ is the state of being greater than any finite real or natural number, however large.
   a. Thing
   b. Infinite0
   c. Undefined
   d. Undefined

91. In set theory, an _____ is a set that is not a finite set. Infinite sets may be countable or uncountable.
   a. Infinite set0
   b. Thing
   c. Undefined
   d. Undefined

92. A _____ is a polynomial function of the form $f(x) = ax^2 + bx + c$, where a, b, c are real numbers and a , 0.
   a. Quadratic function0
   b. Event
   c. Undefined
   d. Undefined

93. The mathematical concept of a _____ expresses the intuitive idea of deterministic dependence between two quantities, one of which is viewed as primary and the other as secondary. A _____ then is a way to associate a unique output for each input of a specified type, for example, a real number or an element of a given set.
   a. Function0
   b. Thing
   c. Undefined
   d. Undefined

94. A _____ is a first degree polynomial mathematical function of the form: $f(x) = mx + b$ where m and b are real constants and x is a real variable.
   a. Linear function0
   b. Thing
   c. Undefined
   d. Undefined

95. The _____ of a ring R is defined to be the smallest positive integer n such that $n\, a = 0$, for all a in R.
   a. Thing
   b. Characteristic0
   c. Undefined
   d. Undefined

Chapter 8. Quadratic Equations and Inequalities

96. In mathematics, the _____ is a conic section generated by the intersection of a right circular conical surface and a plane parallel to a generating straight line of that surface. It can also be defined as locus of points in a plane which are equidistant from a given point.
   a. Thing
   b. Parabola0
   c. Undefined
   d. Undefined

97. An _____ is a collection of two not necessarily distinct objects, one of which is distinguished as the first coordinate and the other as the second coordinate.
   a. Ordered pair0
   b. Thing
   c. Undefined
   d. Undefined

98. In mathematics, the conjugate _____ or adjoint matrix of an m-by-n matrix A with complex entries is the n-by-m matrix A* obtained from A by taking the transpose and then taking the complex conjugate of each entry.
   a. Pairs0
   b. Thing
   c. Undefined
   d. Undefined

99. In mathematics, a _____ of a k-place relation $L \subseteq X_1 \times ... \times X_k$ is one of the sets X_j, $1 \leq j \leq k$. In the special case where k = 2 and $L \subseteq X_1 \times X_2$ is a function $L : X_1 \rightarrow X_2$, it is conventional to refer to X_1 as the _____ of the function and to refer to X_2 as the codomain of the function.
   a. Thing
   b. Domain0
   c. Undefined
   d. Undefined

100. In mathematics, an _____ is any of the arguments, i.e. "inputs", to a function. Thus if we have a function f(x), then x is a _____.
   a. Independent variable0
   b. Thing
   c. Undefined
   d. Undefined

101. _____ are external two-dimensional outlines, with the appearance or configuration of some thing - in contrast to the matter or content or substance of which it is composed.
   a. Thing
   b. Shapes0
   c. Undefined
   d. Undefined

102. In geometry, a _____ is a special kind of point, usually a corner of a polygon, polyhedron, or higher dimensional polytope. In the geometry of curves a _____ is a point of where the first derivative of curvature is zero. In graph theory, a _____ is the fundamental unit out of which graphs are formed
   a. Vertex0
   b. Thing
   c. Undefined
   d. Undefined

103. _____ means "constancy", i.e. if something retains a certain feature even after we change a way of looking at it, then it is symmetric.
   a. Thing
   b. Symmetry0
   c. Undefined
   d. Undefined

104. An _____ is a straight line around which a geometric figure can be rotated.

Chapter 8. Quadratic Equations and Inequalities

a. Axis0
b. Thing
c. Undefined
d. Undefined

105. _____ of a two-dimensional figure is a line such that, if a perpendicular is constructed, any two points lying on the perpendicular at equal distances from the _____ are identical.
   a. Axis of symmetry0
   b. Thing
   c. Undefined
   d. Undefined

106. In mathematics and its applications, a _____ is a system for assigning an n-tuple of numbers or scalars to each point in an n-dimensional space.
   a. Coordinate system0
   b. Concept
   c. Undefined
   d. Undefined

107. In linear algebra, the _____ of an n-by-n square matrix A is defined to be the sum of the elements on the main diagonal of A,
   a. Trace0
   b. Thing
   c. Undefined
   d. Undefined

108. In mathematics, the _____ of a function is the set of all "output" values produced by that function. Given a function $f : A \to B$, the _____ of f, is defined to be the set $\{x \in B : x = f(a) \text{ for some } a \in A\}$.
   a. Range0
   b. Thing
   c. Undefined
   d. Undefined

109. Any point where a graph makes contact with an coordinate axis is called an _____ of the graph
   a. Thing
   b. Intercept0
   c. Undefined
   d. Undefined

110. In mathematics, the _____ of a coordinate system is the point where the axes of the system intersect.
   a. Origin0
   b. Thing
   c. Undefined
   d. Undefined

111. A _____ consists of one quarter of the coordinate plane.
   a. Thing
   b. Quadrant0
   c. Undefined
   d. Undefined

112. In elementary algebra, an _____ is a set that contains every real number between two indicated numbers and may contain the two numbers themselves.
   a. Thing
   b. Interval0
   c. Undefined
   d. Undefined

113. _____ is the distance around a given two-dimensional object. As a general rule, the _____ of a polygon can always be calculated by adding all the length of the sides together. So, the formula for triangles is $P = a + b + c$, where a, b and c stand for each side of it. For quadrilaterals the equation is $P = a + b + c + d$. For equilateral polygons, $P = na$, where n is the number of sides and a is the side length.

Chapter 8. Quadratic Equations and Inequalities

    a. Perimeter0
    c. Undefined
    b. Thing
    d. Undefined

114. _____, from Latin meaning "to make progress", is defined in two different ways. Pure economic _____ is the increase in wealth that an investor has from making an investment, taking into consideration all costs associated with that investment including the opportunity cost of capital.
    a. Thing
    c. Undefined
    b. Profit0
    d. Undefined

115. A _____ is a landform that extends above the surrounding terrain in a limited area. A _____ is generally steeper than a hill, but there is no universally accepted standard definition for the height of a _____ or a hill although a _____ usually has an identifiable summit.
    a. Thing
    c. Undefined
    b. Mountain0
    d. Undefined

116. In astronomy, geography, geometry and related sciences and contexts, a plane is said to be _____ at a given point if it is locally perpendicular to the gradient of the gravity field, i.e., with the direction of the gravitational force at that point.
    a. Horizontal0
    c. Undefined
    b. Thing
    d. Undefined

117. In mathematics, a _____ is a mathematical statement which appears likely to be true, but has not been formally proven to be true under the rules of mathematical logic.
    a. Conjecture0
    c. Undefined
    b. Concept
    d. Undefined

118. _____ is electromagnetic radiation with a wavelength that is visible to the eye (visible _____) or, in a technical or scientific context, electromagnetic radiation of any wavelength.
    a. Thing
    c. Undefined
    b. Light0
    d. Undefined

119. In mathematics, the _____ of two sets A and B is the set that contains all elements of A that also belong to B (or equivalently, all elements of B that also belong to A), but no other elements.
    a. Intersection0
    c. Undefined
    b. Thing
    d. Undefined

120. _____ is a synonym for information.
    a. Thing
    c. Undefined
    b. Data0
    d. Undefined

121. _____ is a way of expressing a number as a fraction of 100 per cent meaning "per hundred".
    a. Thing
    c. Undefined
    b. Percent0
    d. Undefined

122. Deductive _____ is the kind of _____ in which the conclusion is necessitated by, or reached from, previously known facts (the premises).

118   *Chapter 8. Quadratic Equations and Inequalities*

    a. Reasoning0
    b. Thing
    c. Undefined
    d. Undefined

123.   In statistics, a _____ measure is one which is measuring what is supposed to measure.
    a. Thing
    b. Valid0
    c. Undefined
    d. Undefined

124.   In mathematics, for a statement to be mathematically _____, such a statement must be true of all natural numbers.
    a. Inductive0
    b. Thing
    c. Undefined
    d. Undefined

125.   Induction or _____, sometimes called inductive logic, is the process of reasoning in which the premises of an argument are believed to support the conclusion but do not ensure it.
    a. Inductive reasoning0
    b. Thing
    c. Undefined
    d. Undefined

126.   In mathematics, a _____ is an ordered list of objects. Like a set, it contains members, also called elements or terms, and the number of terms is called the length of the _____. Unlike a set, order matters, and the exact same elements can appear multiple times at different positions in the _____.
    a. Thing
    b. Sequence0
    c. Undefined
    d. Undefined

127.   _____ is a natural number that has exactly two distinct natural number divisors, which are 1 and the _____ itself.
    a. Prime number0
    b. Thing
    c. Undefined
    d. Undefined

128.   In mathematics, a _____ number (or a _____) is a natural number that has exactly two (distinct) natural number divisors, which are 1 and the _____ number itself.
    a. Prime0
    b. Thing
    c. Undefined
    d. Undefined

129.   In mathematics, a _____ is a demonstration that, assuming certain axioms, some statement is necessarily true.
    a. Thing
    b. Proof0
    c. Undefined
    d. Undefined

130.   _____ is a method of mathematical proof typically used to establish that a given statement is true of all natural numbers
    a. Mathematical induction0
    b. Thing
    c. Undefined
    d. Undefined

131.   A _____ is one of the basic shapes of geometry: a polygon with three vertices and three sides which are straight line segments.

Chapter 8. Quadratic Equations and Inequalities

a. Thing
b. Triangle0
c. Undefined
d. Undefined

132. A _____ is a function that assigns a number to subsets of a given set.
a. Thing
b. Measure0
c. Undefined
d. Undefined

133. An _____ is an angle formed by two sides of a simple polygon that share an endpoint, namely, the angle on the inner side of the polygon.
a. Thing
b. Interior angle0
c. Undefined
d. Undefined

134. In common philosophical language, a proposition or _____, is the content of an assertion, that is, it is true-or-false and defined by the meaning of a particular piece of language.
a. Concept
b. Statement0
c. Undefined
d. Undefined

135. In a mathematical proof or a syllogism, a _____ is a statement that is the logical consequence of preceding statements.
a. Concept
b. Conclusion0
c. Undefined
d. Undefined

136. Mathematical _____ are demonstrations that, assuming certain axioms, some statement is necessarily true.
a. Proofs0
b. Thing
c. Undefined
d. Undefined

137. In mathematics, a _____ is a statement that can be proved on the basis of explicitly stated or previously agreed assumptions.
a. Theorem0
b. Thing
c. Undefined
d. Undefined

138. _____ is a business term for the amount of money that a company receives from its activities in a given period, mostly from sales of products and/or services to customers
a. Thing
b. Revenue0
c. Undefined
d. Undefined

139. In a company, _____ is the sum of all financial records of salaries, wages, bonuses, and deductions.
a. Thing
b. Payroll0
c. Undefined
d. Undefined

140. _____ is a term used in accounting, economics and finance with reference to the fact that assets with finite lives lose value over time.
a. Thing
b. Depreciation0
c. Undefined
d. Undefined

Chapter 8. Quadratic Equations and Inequalities

141. In finance and economics, _____ is the process of finding the present value of an amount of cash at some future date, and along with compounding cash forms the basis of time value of money calculations.
   a. Thing
   b. Discount0
   c. Undefined
   d. Undefined

142. In Euclidean geometry, a _____ is moving every point a constant distance in a specified direction.
   a. Concept
   b. Translation0
   c. Undefined
   d. Undefined

143. Multiple Signal Classification, also known as _____, is an algorithm used for frequency estimation and emitter location.
   a. Music0
   b. Thing
   c. Undefined
   d. Undefined

Chapter 9. Functions and Relations

1. In mathematics, a _____ of a k-place relation $L \subseteq X_1 \times ... \times X_k$ is one of the sets X_j, $1 \leq j \leq k$. In the special case where k = 2 and $L \subseteq X_1 \times X_2$ is a function $L : X_1 \rightarrow X_2$, it is conventional to refer to X_1 as the _____ of the function and to refer to X_2 as the codomain of the function.
   - a. Thing
   - b. Domain0
   - c. Undefined
   - d. Undefined

2. _____ are the basic objects of study in graph theory. Informally speaking, a graph is a set of objects called points, nodes, or vertices connected by links called lines or edges.
   - a. Thing
   - b. Graphs0
   - c. Undefined
   - d. Undefined

3. In mathematics, the concept of a _____ tries to capture the intuitive idea of a geometrical one-dimensional and continuous object. A simple example is the circle.
   - a. Thing
   - b. Curve0
   - c. Undefined
   - d. Undefined

4. An _____ is a collection of two not necessarily distinct objects, one of which is distinguished as the first coordinate and the other as the second coordinate.
   - a. Thing
   - b. Ordered pair0
   - c. Undefined
   - d. Undefined

5. In mathematics, the conjugate _____ or adjoint matrix of an m-by-n matrix A with complex entries is the n-by-m matrix A* obtained from A by taking the transpose and then taking the complex conjugate of each entry.
   - a. Thing
   - b. Pairs0
   - c. Undefined
   - d. Undefined

6. The mathematical concept of a _____ expresses the intuitive idea of deterministic dependence between two quantities, one of which is viewed as primary and the other as secondary. A _____ then is a way to associate a unique output for each input of a specified type, for example, a real number or an element of a given set.
   - a. Function0
   - b. Thing
   - c. Undefined
   - d. Undefined

7. The _____ of measurement are a globally standardized and modernized form of the metric system.
   - a. Units0
   - b. Thing
   - c. Undefined
   - d. Undefined

8. In mathematics, the _____ (or modulus) of a real number is its numerical value without regard to its sign.
   - a. Thing
   - b. Absolute value0
   - c. Undefined
   - d. Undefined

9. The word _____ comes from the Latin word linearis, which means created by lines.
   - a. Linear0
   - b. Thing
   - c. Undefined
   - d. Undefined

10. In mathematics, a _____ is an expression that is constructed from one or more variables and constants, using only the operations of addition, subtraction, multiplication, and constant positive whole number exponents. is a _____. Note in particular that division by an expression containing a variable is not in general allowed in polynomials. [1]

a. Polynomial0
b. Thing
c. Undefined
d. Undefined

11. _____ is the symbol used to indicate the nth root of a number
   a. Thing
   b. Radical0
   c. Undefined
   d. Undefined

12. A _____ is a number that is less than zero.
   a. Negative number0
   b. Thing
   c. Undefined
   d. Undefined

13. In mathematics, a _____ may be described informally as a number that can be given by an infinite decimal representation.
   a. Thing
   b. Real number0
   c. Undefined
   d. Undefined

14. In plane geometry, a _____ is a polygon with four equal sides, four right angles, and parallel opposite sides. In algebra, the _____ of a number is that number multiplied by itself.
   a. Thing
   b. Square0
   c. Undefined
   d. Undefined

15. In mathematics, a _____ of a number x is a number r such that $r^2 = x$, or in words, a number r whose square (the result of multiplying the number by itself) is x.
   a. Square root0
   b. Thing
   c. Undefined
   d. Undefined

16. In mathematics, an _____ is a statement about the relative size or order of two objects.
   a. Thing
   b. Inequality0
   c. Undefined
   d. Undefined

17. In mathematics, a _____ of a complex-valued function f is a member x of the domain of f such that f(x) vanishes at x, that is, x : f (x) = 0.
   a. Root0
   b. Thing
   c. Undefined
   d. Undefined

18. In mathematics, an inequality is a statement about the relative size or order of two objects. For example 14 > 10, or 14 is _____ 10.
   a. Thing
   b. Greater than0
   c. Undefined
   d. Undefined

19. The _____, the average in everyday English, which is also called the arithmetic _____ (and is distinguished from the geometric _____ or harmonic _____). The average is also called the sample _____. The expected value of a random variable, which is also called the population _____.
   a. Thing
   b. Mean0
   c. Undefined
   d. Undefined

Chapter 9. Functions and Relations

20. A _____ is a set of numbers that designate location in a given reference system, such as x,y in a planar _____ system or an x,y,z in a three-dimensional _____ system.
    a. Coordinate0
    b. Thing
    c. Undefined
    d. Undefined

21. In mathematics, the _____ f is the collection of all ordered pairs . In particular, graph means the graphical representation of this collection, in the form of a curve or surface, together with axes, etc. Graphing on a Cartesian plane is sometimes referred to as curve sketching.
    a. Graph of a function0
    b. Thing
    c. Undefined
    d. Undefined

22. In common philosophical language, a proposition or _____, is the content of an assertion, that is, it is true-or-false and defined by the meaning of a particular piece of language.
    a. Statement0
    b. Concept
    c. Undefined
    d. Undefined

23. _____ is a test to determine if a relation or its graph is a function or not
    a. Vertical line test0
    b. Thing
    c. Undefined
    d. Undefined

24. Acid _____ ratio measures the ability of a company to use its near cash or quick assets to immediately extinguish its current liabilities.
    a. Test0
    b. Thing
    c. Undefined
    d. Undefined

25. In Euclidean geometry, a _____ is the set of all points in a plane at a fixed distance, called the radius, from a given point, the center.
    a. Circle0
    b. Thing
    c. Undefined
    d. Undefined

26. In geometry, an _____ of a triangle is a straight line through a vertex and perpendicular to (i.e. forming a right angle with) the opposite side or an extension of the opposite side.
    a. Concept
    b. Altitude0
    c. Undefined
    d. Undefined

27. _____ is a physical property of a system that underlies the common notions of hot and cold; something that is hotter has the greater _____.
    a. Thing
    b. Temperature0
    c. Undefined
    d. Undefined

28. In mathematics, the _____ of a function is the set of all "output" values produced by that function. Given a function $f : A \to B$, the _____ of f, is defined to be the set $\{x \in B : x = f(a) \text{ for some } a \in A\}$.
    a. Thing
    b. Range0
    c. Undefined
    d. Undefined

29. Mathematical _____ is used to represent ideas.

Chapter 9. Functions and Relations

    a. Notation0   b. Thing
    c. Undefined   d. Undefined

30. In mathematics, _____ geometry was the traditional name for the geometry of three-dimensional Euclidean space — for practical purposes the kind of space we live in.
    a. Solid0   b. Thing
    c. Undefined   d. Undefined

31. _____ the expected value of a random variable displays the average or central value of the variable. It is a summary value of the distribution of the variable.
    a. Determining0   b. Thing
    c. Undefined   d. Undefined

32. In elementary algebra, an _____ is a set that contains every real number between two indicated numbers and may contain the two numbers themselves.
    a. Interval0   b. Thing
    c. Undefined   d. Undefined

33. The _____ is the number or expression underneath the radical sign.
    a. Radicand0   b. Thing
    c. Undefined   d. Undefined

34. In mathematics, a _____ is a mathematical statement which appears likely to be true, but has not been formally proven to be true under the rules of mathematical logic.
    a. Concept   b. Conjecture0
    c. Undefined   d. Undefined

35. In Euclidean geometry, a _____ is moving every point a constant distance in a specified direction.
    a. Concept   b. Translation0
    c. Undefined   d. Undefined

36. In mathematics and the mathematical sciences, a _____ is a fixed, but possibly unspecified, value. This is in contrast to a variable, which is not fixed.
    a. Constant0   b. Thing
    c. Undefined   d. Undefined

37. In astronomy, geography, geometry and related sciences and contexts, a plane is said to be _____ at a given point if it is locally perpendicular to the gradient of the gravity field, i.e., with the direction of the gravitational force at that point.
    a. Horizontal0   b. Thing
    c. Undefined   d. Undefined

38. A _____ is a symbolic representation denoting a quantity or expression. It often represents an "unknown" quantity that has the potential to change.
    a. Variable0   b. Thing
    c. Undefined   d. Undefined

Chapter 9. Functions and Relations

39. In mathematics, _____ is an elementary arithmetic operation. When one of the numbers is a whole number, _____ is the repeated sum of the other number.
   a. Thing
   b. Multiplication0
   c. Undefined
   d. Undefined

40. An _____ is a combination of numbers, operators, grouping symbols and/or free variables and bound variables arranged in a meaningful way which can be evaluated..
   a. Thing
   b. Expression0
   c. Undefined
   d. Undefined

41. _____ is a branch of mathematics concerning the study of structure, relation and quantity.
   a. Concept
   b. Algebra0
   c. Undefined
   d. Undefined

42. In mathematics, a _____ of a positive integer n is a way of writing n as a sum of positive integers.
   a. Composition0
   b. Thing
   c. Undefined
   d. Undefined

43. The _____ functions is determined by the nesting of two or more functions to form a single new function.
   a. Thing
   b. Composition of two0
   c. Undefined
   d. Undefined

44. A _____ number is a positive integer which has a positive divisor other than one or itself.
   a. Composite0
   b. Thing
   c. Undefined
   d. Undefined

45. A _____ is a simplified and structured visual representation of concepts, ideas, constructions, relations, statistical data, anatomy etc used in all aspects of human activities to visualize and clarify the topic.
   a. Diagram0
   b. Thing
   c. Undefined
   d. Undefined

46. A _____, formed by the composition of one function on another, represents the application of the former to the result of the application of the latter to the argument of the composite.
   a. Composite function0
   b. Thing
   c. Undefined
   d. Undefined

47. _____ element of an element x with respect to a binary operation * with identity element e is an element y such that x * y = y * x = e. In particular,
   a. Inverse0
   b. Thing
   c. Undefined
   d. Undefined

48. In mathematics, in the field of group theory, a _____ of a group is a quasisimple subnormal subgroup.
   a. Component0
   b. Concept
   c. Undefined
   d. Undefined

49. An _____ is a function which does the reverse of a given function.

Chapter 9. Functions and Relations

    a. Inverse function0
    b. Thing
    c. Undefined
    d. Undefined

50. _____ is a test used to determine if a function is injective, surjective or bijective.
    a. Thing
    b. Horizontal line test0
    c. Undefined
    d. Undefined

51. A _____ is a polynomial function of the form $f(x) = ax^2 + bx + c$, where a, b, c are real numbers and a , 0.
    a. Quadratic function0
    b. Event
    c. Undefined
    d. Undefined

52. In mathematics, the multiplicative inverse of a number x, denoted 1/x or x^{-1}, is the number which, when multiplied by x, yields 1. The multiplicative inverse of x is also called the _____ of x.
    a. Thing
    b. Reciprocal0
    c. Undefined
    d. Undefined

53. In mathematics, _____ is a part of the set theoretic notion of function.
    a. Image0
    b. Thing
    c. Undefined
    d. Undefined

54. A _____ is 360° or 2δ radians.
    a. Turn0
    b. Thing
    c. Undefined
    d. Undefined

55. A _____ signifies a point or points of probability on a subject e.g., the _____ of creativity, which allows for the formation of rule or norm or law by interpretation of the phenomena events that can be created.
    a. Principle0
    b. Thing
    c. Undefined
    d. Undefined

56. _____ forms part of thinking. Considered the most complex of all intellectual functions, _____ has been defined as higher-order cognitive process that requires the modulation and control of more routine or fundamental skills.
    a. Problem solving0
    b. Thing
    c. Undefined
    d. Undefined

57. In mathematics, a _____ is a demonstration that, assuming certain axioms, some statement is necessarily true.
    a. Proof0
    b. Thing
    c. Undefined
    d. Undefined

58. A _____ is a first degree polynomial mathematical function of the form: $f(x) = mx + b$ where m and b are real constants and x is a real variable.
    a. Thing
    b. Linear function0
    c. Undefined
    d. Undefined

59. Mathematical _____ really refers to two distinct areas of research: the first is the application of the techniques of formal _____ to mathematics and mathematical reasoning, and the second, in the other direction, the application of mathematical techniques to the representation and analysis of formal _____.

Chapter 9. Functions and Relations

    a. Thing
    b. Logic0
    c. Undefined
    d. Undefined

60. _____ was a Greek philosopher, a student of Plato and teacher of Alexander the Great. He wrote on diverse subjects, including physics, metaphysics, poetry, biology and zoology, logic, rhetoric, politics, government, and ethics.
    a. Aristotle0
    b. Person
    c. Undefined
    d. Undefined

61. In mathematics, a _____ is an ordered list of objects. Like a set, it contains members, also called elements or terms, and the number of terms is called the length of the _____. Unlike a set, order matters, and the exact same elements can appear multiple times at different positions in the _____.
    a. Sequence0
    b. Thing
    c. Undefined
    d. Undefined

62. In mathematics, a _____ is the result of multiplying, or an expression that identifies factors to be multiplied.
    a. Thing
    b. Product0
    c. Undefined
    d. Undefined

63. In mathematics, the _____ inverse, or opposite, of a number n is the number that, when added to n, yields zero. The _____ inverse of n is denoted −n.
    a. Additive0
    b. Thing
    c. Undefined
    d. Undefined

64. In mathematics, the _____ of a number n is the number that, when added to n, yields zero. The _____ of n is denoted −n. For example, 7 is −7, because 7 + (−7) = 0, and the _____ of −0.3 is 0.3, because −0.3 + 0.3 = 0.
    a. Thing
    b. Additive inverse0
    c. Undefined
    d. Undefined

65. In mathematics, and in particular in abstract algebra, the _____ is a property of binary operations that generalises the distributive law from elementary algebra.
    a. Distributive property0
    b. Thing
    c. Undefined
    d. Undefined

66. _____ is a relation in Euclidean geometry among the three sides of a right triangle.
    a. Thing
    b. Pythagorean Theorem0
    c. Undefined
    d. Undefined

67. In mathematics, a _____ is a statement that can be proved on the basis of explicitly stated or previously agreed assumptions.
    a. Thing
    b. Theorem0
    c. Undefined
    d. Undefined

68. A _____ is one of the basic shapes of geometry: a polygon with three vertices and three sides which are straight line segments.

Chapter 9. Functions and Relations

    a. Thing
    b. Triangle0
    c. Undefined
    d. Undefined

69. _____ has one 90° internal angle a right angle.
    a. Right triangle0
    b. Thing
    c. Undefined
    d. Undefined

70. A _____ is a quantity that denotes the proportional amount or magnitude of one quantity relative to another.
    a. Thing
    b. Ratio0
    c. Undefined
    d. Undefined

71. In a right triangle, the _____ of the triangle are the two sides that are perpendicular to each other, as opposed to the hypotenuse.
    a. Legs0
    b. Thing
    c. Undefined
    d. Undefined

72. The _____ of a right triangle is the triangle's longest side; the side opposite the right angle.
    a. Thing
    b. Hypotenuse0
    c. Undefined
    d. Undefined

73. _____ is the application of tools and a processing medium to the transformation of raw materials into finished goods for sale.
    a. Thing
    b. Manufacturing0
    c. Undefined
    d. Undefined

74. In finance and economics, _____ is the process of finding the present value of an amount of cash at some future date, and along with compounding cash forms the basis of time value of money calculations.
    a. Thing
    b. Discount0
    c. Undefined
    d. Undefined

75. _____ is the notation in which permitted values for a variable are expressed as ranging over a certain interval; "5 < x < 9" is an example of the application of _____.
    a. Thing
    b. Interval notation0
    c. Undefined
    d. Undefined

76. In geometry, a _____ is a special kind of point, usually a corner of a polygon, polyhedron, or higher dimensional polytope. In the geometry of curves a _____ is a point of where the first derivative of curvature is zero. In graph theory, a _____ is the fundamental unit out of which graphs are formed
    a. Thing
    b. Vertex0
    c. Undefined
    d. Undefined

77. _____ means "constancy", i.e. if something retains a certain feature even after we change a way of looking at it, then it is symmetric.
    a. Symmetry0
    b. Thing
    c. Undefined
    d. Undefined

Chapter 9. Functions and Relations

78. An _____ is a straight line around which a geometric figure can be rotated.
 a. Axis0
 b. Thing
 c. Undefined
 d. Undefined

79. _____ of a two-dimensional figure is a line such that, if a perpendicular is constructed, any two points lying on the perpendicular at equal distances from the _____ are identical.
 a. Thing
 b. Axis of symmetry0
 c. Undefined
 d. Undefined

80. In chemistry, a _____ is substance made by combining two or more different materials in such a way that no chemical reaction occurs.
 a. Thing
 b. Mixture0
 c. Undefined
 d. Undefined

81. In statistics the _____ of an event i is the number n_i of times the event occurred in the experiment or the study. These frequencies are often graphically represented in histograms.
 a. Frequency0
 b. Concept
 c. Undefined
 d. Undefined

82. _____ is the scientific study of celestial objects such as stars, planets, comets, and galaxies; and phenomena that originate outside the Earth's atmosphere.
 a. Astronomy0
 b. Thing
 c. Undefined
 d. Undefined

83. _____ is a radiometric dating method that uses the naturally occurring isotope carbon-14 to determine the age of carbonaceous materials up to about 60,000 years.
 a. Radiocarbon dating0
 b. Thing
 c. Undefined
 d. Undefined

84. The payment of _____ as remuneration for services rendered or products sold is a common way to reward sales people.
 a. Commission0
 b. Thing
 c. Undefined
 d. Undefined

85. A _____ is a type of debt. All material things can be lent but this article focuses exclusively on monetary loans. Like all debt instruments, a _____ entails the redistribution of financial assets over time, between the lender and the borrower.
 a. Thing
 b. Loan0
 c. Undefined
 d. Undefined

86. A _____ is a special kind of ratio, indicating a relationship between two measurements with different units, such as miles to gallons or cents to pounds.
 a. Rate0
 b. Thing
 c. Undefined
 d. Undefined

87. _____ is a way of expressing a number as a fraction of 100 per cent meaning "per hundred".

a. Thing
b. Percent0
c. Undefined
d. Undefined

88. _____, Greek for "knowledge of nature," is the branch of science concerned with the discovery and characterization of universal laws which govern matter, energy, space, and time.
a. Thing
b. Physics0
c. Undefined
d. Undefined

Chapter 10. Exponential and Logarithmic Functions

1. <U>Twice</U> means to multiply by 2.
   a. Twice10
   b. -equivalence
   c. Undefined
   d. Undefined

2. A number that is raised to a power, or _____ of an exponential function. This finds common use, for example, in the depiction of numbers, for instance, 10 is the _____ used in the decimal system, whereas 2 is the _____ in the binary numeral system.
   a. -equivalence
   b. Base10
   c. Undefined
   d. Undefined

3. When a number in decimal form does not repeat nor terminate, it is an <U>irrational number</U>. Pi and the square root of 7 are example s of an _____.
   a. Irrational number10
   b. ADE classification
   c. Undefined
   d. Undefined

4. _____, or less commonly, denary, usually refers to the base 10 numeral system.
   a. Decimal10
   b. -equivalence
   c. Undefined
   d. Undefined

5. The word _____ can have three meanings: In _____ theory, a _____ is an abstract object consisting of vertices (or nodes) and edges (or arcs) between pairs of vertices. The _____ of a function f : X ¨ Y is the set of all pairs (x,f(x)) The _____ of a relation, a generalisation of the _____ of a function.
   a. -equivalence
   b. Graph10
   c. Undefined
   d. Undefined

6. An <U>equation</U> is represented by two expressions that have the same value.
   a. Equation10
   b. ADE classification
   c. Undefined
   d. Undefined

7. The _____ is the point where a graph intersects the x-axis and is found by letting y = 0 and then solving for the x-value.
   a. X-intercept10
   b. -equivalence
   c. Undefined
   d. Undefined

8. A <U>point </U>is an undefined term. We usually represent this by a dot, but a _____ actually has no dimension. A capital letter names any _____.
   a. Point10
   b. -equivalence
   c. Undefined
   d. Undefined

9. The <U>exponent </U>indicates how many of the base to multiply together to get the product. When 5 to the third power is 125, then 3 is the _____ and can also be called a power.
   a. Exponent10
   b. ADE classification
   c. Undefined
   d. Undefined

10. When a number is written with an exponent this number will be in <U>exponential form.</U>

a. Exponential form10   b. ADE classification
c. Undefined   d. Undefined

11. An irrational number is any real number that is not a rational number, i.e., one that cannot be written as a ratio of two integers, i.e., it is not of the form a/b where a and b are integers and b is not zero. It can readily be shown that the _____ are precisely those numbers whose expansion in any given base (decimal, binary, etc) never ends and never enters a periodic pattern, but no mathematician takes that to be a definition. Almost all real numbers are irrational, in a sense which is defined more precisely below. Some _____ are algebraic numbers, such as ã2, the square root of two, and 3 ã5, the cube root of 5; others are transcendental numbers such as fÎ and e.

a. Irrational numbers10   b. ADE classification
c. Undefined   d. Undefined

12. One <U>expanded form </U>is found when simplifying an exponential expression. Given 4<supɯ</sup>, it can now be rewritten in _____: 4 x 4 x 4

a. ADE classification   b. Expanded form10
c. Undefined   d. Undefined

13. Another word for independent variables in the analysis of variance is _____.

a. Factors10   b. -equivalence
c. Undefined   d. Undefined

14. A _____ is the result of multiplying, or an expression that identifies factors to be multiplied

a. -equivalence   b. Product10
c. Undefined   d. Undefined

15. A _____ is the end result of a division problem. For example, in the problem 6 ÷ 3, the _____ would be 2, while 6 would be called the dividend, and 3 the divisor

a. Quotient10   b. -equivalence
c. Undefined   d. Undefined

16. An _____ combines numbers, operators, and/or variables but contains no equal or inequality sign.

a. Expression10   b. ADE classification
c. Undefined   d. Undefined

17. _____ are intuitively defined as numbers that are in one-to-one correspondence with the points on an infinite line—the number line. The term "real number" is a retronym coined in response to "imaginary number" _____ may be rational or irrational; algebraic or transcendental; and positive, negative, or zero _____ measure continuous quantities. They may in theory be expressed by decimal fractions that have an infinite sequence of digits to the right of the decimal point; these are often (mis-)represented in the same form as 324.823211247... (where the three dots express that there would still be more digits to come, no matter how many more might be added at the end).

a. Real numbers10   b. -equivalence
c. Undefined   d. Undefined

18. An _____ is a variable, constant, or any combination that contains an exponent. Examples are 3<supɮ</sup>, x<supɯ</sup>, and 4x<supɮ</sup>,

Chapter 10. Exponential and Logarithmic Functions

a. Exponential expression10
c. Undefined
b. ADE classification
d. Undefined

19. The probability of correctly rejecting a false Ho is referred to as _____.
    a. -equivalence
    c. Undefined
    b. Power10
    d. Undefined

20. A _____ is a multiplicative factor of a certain object such as a variable (for example, the coefficients of a polynomial), a basis vector, a basis function and so on. Usually, the objects and the coefficients are indexed in the same way, leading to expressions such as a1x1 + a2x2 + a3x3 + ... where an is the _____ of the variable xn for each n = 1, 2, 3, ...
    a. -equivalence
    c. Undefined
    b. Coefficient10
    d. Undefined

21. A _____ is an undefined term. However, it is often thought of as a series of points. A _____ has one dimension - length. A _____ is either named by a lower case letter or by two points on the _____.
    a. Line10
    c. Undefined
    b. -equivalence
    d. Undefined

22. By _____ we mean collecting observations made upon our environment -- observations, which are the results of measurements using clocks, balances, measuring rods, counting operations, or other objectively defined measuring instruments or procedures. _____ may mean simply counting the number of times a particular property occurs.
    a. -equivalence
    c. Undefined
    b. Data10
    d. Undefined

23. A percentage is a way of expressing a proportion, a ratio or a fraction as a whole number, by using 100 as the denominator. A number such as "45%" ("45 percent" or "45 per cent") is shorthand for the fraction 45/100 or 0.45.As an illustration,"45 _____ of human beings..." is equivalent to both of the following:"45 out of every 100 people..." "0.45 of the human population..." One way to think about percentages is to realize that "one percent", represented by the symbol %, is simply the number 1/100, or 0.01.
    a. Percent10
    c. Undefined
    b. -equivalence
    d. Undefined

24. A _____ is a number or variable, or the product or quotient of a number or variable.
    a. -equivalence
    c. Undefined
    b. Term10
    d. Undefined

25. The very fact that we are measuring objects with respect to some characteristic implies that the objects differ in that characteristic; or stated in another way, that the characteristic can take on a number of different values. These properties or characteristics of an object that can assume two or more different values are referred to as a _____.
    a. Variable10
    c. Undefined
    b. -equivalence
    d. Undefined

26. An _____ is an indication of the value of an unknown quantity based on observed data. More formally, an _____ is the particular value of an estimator that is obtained from a particular sample of data and used to indicate the value of a parameter.

Chapter 10. Exponential and Logarithmic Functions

    a. Estimate10   b. ADE classification
    c. Undefined   d. Undefined

27. The _____ are on the right of the zero on the number line. Although they can have the + sign, it is usually left out.
    a. -equivalence   b. Positive numbers10
    c. Undefined   d. Undefined

28. If one number is to the right of another number on the number line, this number is <U>greater than </U>the number on the left. The symbol that is used is >.
    a. Greater than10   b. -equivalence
    c. Undefined   d. Undefined

29. A _____ is a scheme for the numerical representation of the values of a variable. The interpretation we place upon the numbers of the _____, rather than the numbers themselves, makes the _____ useful. The most common scales are nominal, ordinal, interval
    a. -equivalence   b. Scale10
    c. Undefined   d. Undefined

30. A number that does not change in value in a given situation is a _____.
    a. Constant10   b. -equivalence
    c. Undefined   d. Undefined

31. A _____ is a subset or portion of a population. Samples are extremely important in the field of statistical analysis, since due to economic and practical constraints we usually cannot make measurements on every single member of the particular population.
    a. -equivalence   b. Sample10
    c. Undefined   d. Undefined

32. A quadrilateral with 4 equal sides and all right angles is called a <U>square.</U>
    a. Square10   b. -equivalence
    c. Undefined   d. Undefined

33. The answer to subtraction is called the <U>difference</U>.
    a. Difference10   b. -equivalence
    c. Undefined   d. Undefined

34. A <U>quadratic</U> contains at least one squared term.
    a. -equivalence   b. Quadratic10
    c. Undefined   d. Undefined

35. a <U>rational number </U>(or informally fraction) is a ratio or quotient of two integers, usually written as the fraction a/b, where b is not zero. Each _____ can be written in infinitely many forms, for example 3 / 6 = 2 / 4 = 1 / 2. When rational numbers are turned into the decimal equivalents the numbers eventually end or repeat.
    a. Rational number10   b. -equivalence
    c. Undefined   d. Undefined

Chapter 10. Exponential and Logarithmic Functions

36. A _____ is the relationship between two quantities. It is expressed as the quotient of two numbers, or as two numbers separated by a colon (pronounced "to"). A number that can be written as a _____ of two integers is a rational number.
   a. Ratio10
   b. -equivalence
   c. Undefined
   d. Undefined

37. A triangle with all sides of equal length is called an <U>equilateral triangle</U>.
   a. ADE classification
   b. Equilateral triangle10
   c. Undefined
   d. Undefined

38. Any polygon that has 3 sides is called a <U>triangle</U>.
   a. -equivalence
   b. Triangle10
   c. Undefined
   d. Undefined

39. A measure of variability, the _____ is the distance from the lowest to the highest score.
   a. -equivalence
   b. Range10
   c. Undefined
   d. Undefined

40. The lowest number in a list of values is called the <U>minimum</U>.
   a. -equivalence
   b. Minimum10
   c. Undefined
   d. Undefined

41. A _____ is a concrete example of an item or a specification against which all others may be measured. For example, there are "primary standards" for length, mass (see Kilogram standard), and other units of measure, kept by laboratories and standards organizations.
   a. -equivalence
   b. Standard10
   c. Undefined
   d. Undefined

42. One number is <U>divisible by </U>another number if division is completed without a remainder. Since 8 is _____ 2, we say 8 is _____ 2.
   a. -equivalence
   b. Divisible by10
   c. Undefined
   d. Undefined

Chapter 11. Sequences and Series

1. A _____ is a number or variable, or the product or quotient of a number or variable.
   a. -equivalence
   b. Term11
   c. Undefined
   d. Undefined

2. A _____ is a positive integer (1,2,3,...).
   a. -equivalence
   b. Natural number11
   c. Undefined
   d. Undefined

3. Addition (or summation) is one of the basic operations of arithmetic. In its simplest form, addition combines two numbers, the augend and addend, into a single number, the _____. Adding more numbers can be viewed as repeated addition. (Repeated addition of the number one is the most basic form of counting.) By extension, the addition of zero numbers, one number, or infinitely many numbers can be defined.
   a. -equivalence
   b. Sum11
   c. Undefined
   d. Undefined

4. The Greek letter _____ indicates summation.
   a. Sigma11
   b. -equivalence
   c. Undefined
   d. Undefined

5. _____ or arithmetics (from the Greek word áñééìüò = number) in common usage is a branch of (or the forerunner of) mathematics which records elementary properties of certain operations on numerals, though in usage by professional mathematicians, it often is treated as a synonym for number theory.
   a. Arithmetic11
   b. ADE classification
   c. Undefined
   d. Undefined

6. A number that does not change in value in a given situation is a _____.
   a. Constant11
   b. -equivalence
   c. Undefined
   d. Undefined

7. The answer to subtraction is called the <U>difference</U>.
   a. Difference11
   b. -equivalence
   c. Undefined
   d. Undefined

8. Any time one number is on the left side of another number on a number line, the first number is <U>less than </U>the second number. The symbol for this is <.
   a. Less than11
   b. -equivalence
   c. Undefined
   d. Undefined

9. At times we must contend with variables that assume a large number of values. In this case it is typical to create _____ of values of the variable and then make a frequency tally of the number of observations falling within each interval. As is the case with any data reduction technique, detail is lost.
   a. Intervals11
   b. ADE classification
   c. Undefined
   d. Undefined

10. _____ refer to any data source, whether individuals, physical or biological things, geographic locations, time periods, or events; that is, anything upon which observations can be made.

Chapter 11. Sequences and Series

a. ADE classification
b. Objects11
c. Undefined
d. Undefined

11. A _____ is a multiplicative factor of a certain object such as a variable (for example, the coefficients of a polynomial), a basis vector, a basis function and so on. Usually, the objects and the coefficients are indexed in the same way, leading to expressions such as $a_1 x_1 + a_2 x_2 + a_3 x_3 + \ldots$ where a_n is the _____ of the variable x_n for each $n = 1, 2, 3, \ldots$

a. -equivalence
b. Coefficient11
c. Undefined
d. Undefined

12. _____ (from the Greek words Geo = earth and metro = measure) is the branch of mathematics first popularized in ancient Greek culture by Thales (circa 624-547 BC) dealing with spatial relationships. The earliest beginnings of _____ may be traced to Ancient Egypt

a. Geometry11
b. -equivalence
c. Undefined
d. Undefined

13. Any polygon that has 3 sides is called a <U>triangle</U>.

a. Triangle11
b. -equivalence
c. Undefined
d. Undefined

14. A five sided polygon is called a <U>pentagon</U>.

a. Pentagon11
b. -equivalence
c. Undefined
d. Undefined

15. Any polygon with 4 sides is called a <U>quadrilateral</U>. The sum of the interior angles is 360 degrees.

a. -equivalence
b. Quadrilateral11
c. Undefined
d. Undefined

16. A closed shape whose sides are all line segments is called a <U>polygon.</U>

a. -equivalence
b. Polygon11
c. Undefined
d. Undefined

17. A _____ is a well-defined collection of objects considered as a whole.

a. Set11
b. -equivalence
c. Undefined
d. Undefined

18. _____ is an estimate of the decrease in the value of an asset, caused by "wear and tear", obsolescence, or impairment. The use of _____ affects a company's (or an individual's) financial statements, and, in some countries, their taxes.

a. -equivalence
b. Depreciation11
c. Undefined
d. Undefined

19. An <U>equation</U> is represented by two expressions that have the same value.

a. ADE classification
b. Equation11
c. Undefined
d. Undefined

Chapter 11. Sequences and Series

20. An _____ combines numbers, operators, and/or variables but contains no equal or inequality sign.
    a. Expression11
    b. ADE classification
    c. Undefined
    d. Undefined

21. A _____ is a subset or portion of a population. Samples are extremely important in the field of statistical analysis, since due to economic and practical constraints we usually cannot make measurements on every single member of the particular population.
    a. Sample11
    b. -equivalence
    c. Undefined
    d. Undefined

22. A _____ is an undefined term. However, it is often thought of as a series of points. A _____ has one dimension - length. A _____ is either named by a lower case letter or by two points on the _____.
    a. -equivalence
    b. Line11
    c. Undefined
    d. Undefined

23. When a given number is multiplied by any or all natural numbers, <U>multiples</U> are formed. 2, 4, 6 are all examples of multiples of 2.
    a. -equivalence
    b. Multiple11
    c. Undefined
    d. Undefined

24. A _____ is the relationship between two quantities. It is expressed as the quotient of two numbers, or as two numbers separated by a colon (pronounced "to"). A number that can be written as a _____ of two integers is a rational number.
    a. Ratio11
    b. -equivalence
    c. Undefined
    d. Undefined

25. The <U>exponent </U>indicates how many of the base to multiply together to get the product. When 5 to the third power is 125, then 3 is the _____ and can also be called a power.
    a. Exponent11
    b. ADE classification
    c. Undefined
    d. Undefined

26. _____ is the study of quantity, structure, space, and change. Historically, _____ developed from counting, calculation, measurement, and the study of the shapes and motions of physical objects, through the use of abstraction and deductive reasoning.
    a. -equivalence
    b. Mathematics11
    c. Undefined
    d. Undefined

27. A quadrilateral with 4 equal sides and all right angles is called a <U>square.</U>
    a. -equivalence
    b. Square11
    c. Undefined
    d. Undefined

28. _____, or less commonly, denary, usually refers to the base 10 numeral system.
    a. Decimal11
    b. -equivalence
    c. Undefined
    d. Undefined

29. A _____ is a quotient of numbers, like 3⁄4, or more generally, an element of a quotient field.

Chapter 11. Sequences and Series

a. Fraction11	b. -equivalence
c. Undefined	d. Undefined

30. A piece of a circle is called an <U>arc.</U>

a. Arc11	b. ADE classification
c. Undefined	d. Undefined

31. _____ is the result of assigning numbers to objects to abstractly represent the objects or characteristics of the objects.

a. -equivalence	b. Measurement11
c. Undefined	d. Undefined

32. A triangle with all sides of equal length is called an <U>equilateral triangle</U>.

a. Equilateral triangle11	b. ADE classification
c. Undefined	d. Undefined

33. A _____ is simply a polynomial with two terms such as this example: 2x + 7.

a. -equivalence	b. Binomial11
c. Undefined	d. Undefined

34. Another word for independent variables in the analysis of variance is _____.

a. -equivalence	b. Factors11
c. Undefined	d. Undefined

35. The number that is divided into is called the <U>dividend.</U> When 6 is divided by 2, 6 is called the _____.

a. Dividend11	b. -equivalence
c. Undefined	d. Undefined

36. If one number is to the right of another number on the number line, this number is <U>greater than </U>the number on the left. The symbol that is used is >.

a. -equivalence	b. Greater than11
c. Undefined	d. Undefined

37. A percentage is a way of expressing a proportion, a ratio or a fraction as a whole number, by using 100 as the denominator. A number such as "45%" ("45 percent" or "45 per cent") is shorthand for the fraction 45/100 or 0.45.As an illustration,"45 _____ of human beings..." is equivalent to both of the following:"45 out of every 100 people..." "0.45 of the human population..." One way to think about percentages is to realize that "one percent", represented by the symbol %, is simply the number 1/100, or 0.01.

a. Percent11	b. -equivalence
c. Undefined	d. Undefined

38. _____ is the change in x between two points

a. Run11	b. -equivalence
c. Undefined	d. Undefined

Chapter 11. Sequences and Series

39. A <U>point </U>is an undefined term. We usually represent this by a dot, but a _____ actually has no dimension. A capital letter names any _____.
   a. Point11
   b. -equivalence
   c. Undefined
   d. Undefined

40. The very fact that we are measuring objects with respect to some characteristic implies that the objects differ in that characteristic; or stated in another way, that the characteristic can take on a number of different values. These properties or characteristics of an object that can assume two or more different values are referred to as a _____.
   a. -equivalence
   b. Variable11
   c. Undefined
   d. Undefined

41. A _____ is the result of multiplying, or an expression that identifies factors to be multiplied
   a. -equivalence
   b. Product11
   c. Undefined
   d. Undefined

42. The bottom part of any fraction represents the number of pieces in one whole unit. This bottom part is called the <U>denominator.</U>
   a. -equivalence
   b. Denominator11
   c. Undefined
   d. Undefined

43. One <U>expanded form </U>is found when simplifying an exponential expression. Given 4<supш</sup>, it can now be rewritten in _____: 4 x 4 x 4
   a. Expanded form11
   b. ADE classification
   c. Undefined
   d. Undefined

44. A _____ is a concrete example of an item or a specification against which all others may be measured. For example, there are "primary standards" for length, mass (see Kilogram standard), and other units of measure, kept by laboratories and standards organizations.
   a. -equivalence
   b. Standard11
   c. Undefined
   d. Undefined

Chapter 12. Conic sections

1. The word _____ can have three meanings: In _____ theory, a _____ is an abstract object consisting of vertices (or nodes) and edges (or arcs) between pairs of vertices. The _____ of a function f : X ¨ Y is the set of all pairs (x,f(x)) The _____ of a relation, a generalisation of the _____ of a function.
   a. -equivalence
   b. Graph12
   c. Undefined
   d. Undefined

2. A <U>plane</U> is an undefined term. We can think of it as a series of lines having 2 dimensions, width and length.
   a. -equivalence
   b. Plane12
   c. Undefined
   d. Undefined

3. A <U>circle</U> is a series of points the same distance from a given point, called the center.
   a. -equivalence
   b. Circle12
   c. Undefined
   d. Undefined

4. An <U>axis</U> is one of the number lines found on the rectangular coordinate system. The x asis is the horizontal number line while the y _____ is the vertical number line.
   a. Axis12
   b. ADE classification
   c. Undefined
   d. Undefined

5. _____ is implied when data values are distributed in the same way above and below the middle of the sample.
   a. -equivalence
   b. Symmetry12
   c. Undefined
   d. Undefined

6. An <U>equation</U> is represented by two expressions that have the same value.
   a. Equation12
   b. ADE classification
   c. Undefined
   d. Undefined

7. A <U>point </U>is an undefined term. We usually represent this by a dot, but a _____ actually has no dimension. A capital letter names any _____.
   a. -equivalence
   b. Point12
   c. Undefined
   d. Undefined

8. A quadrilateral with 4 equal sides and all right angles is called a <U>square.</U>
   a. Square12
   b. -equivalence
   c. Undefined
   d. Undefined

9. _____ is used synonymously for variable.
   a. -equivalence
   b. Factor12
   c. Undefined
   d. Undefined

10. A _____ is simply a polynomial with three terms connect by addition and multiplication.
    a. Trinomial12
    b. -equivalence
    c. Undefined
    d. Undefined

Chapter 12. Conic sections

11. A _____ is a multiplicative factor of a certain object such as a variable (for example, the coefficients of a polynomial), a basis vector, a basis function and so on. Usually, the objects and the coefficients are indexed in the same way, leading to expressions such as $a_1x_1 + a_2x_2 + a_3x_3 + ...$ where a_n is the _____ of the variable x_n for each $n = 1, 2, 3, ...$
   a. -equivalence
   b. Coefficient12
   c. Undefined
   d. Undefined

12. A _____ is an undefined term. However, it is often thought of as a series of points. A _____ has one dimension - length. A _____ is either named by a lower case letter or by two points on the _____.
   a. Line12
   b. -equivalence
   c. Undefined
   d. Undefined

13. The point of intersection of the horizontal and vertical axes in the rectangular coordinate plane is the _____. It is is expressed as the ordered pair (0,0).
   a. Origin12
   b. ADE classification
   c. Undefined
   d. Undefined

14. The <U>diameter</U> of a circle is a chord that goes through the center.
   a. -equivalence
   b. Diameter12
   c. Undefined
   d. Undefined

15. By _____ we mean the cumulative frequency, counting in from the nearer end.
   a. Depth12
   b. -equivalence
   c. Undefined
   d. Undefined

16. The <U>radius</U> of a circle is the distance from the center to the circle.
   a. Radius12
   b. -equivalence
   c. Undefined
   d. Undefined

17. A _____ is a concrete example of an item or a specification against which all others may be measured. For example, there are "primary standards" for length, mass (see Kilogram standard), and other units of measure, kept by laboratories and standards organizations.
   a. -equivalence
   b. Standard12
   c. Undefined
   d. Undefined

18. A number that does not change in value in a given situation is a _____.
   a. Constant12
   b. -equivalence
   c. Undefined
   d. Undefined

19. A _____ is a number or variable, or the product or quotient of a number or variable.
   a. -equivalence
   b. Term12
   c. Undefined
   d. Undefined

20. Any time one number is on the left side of another number on a number line, the first number is <U>less than </U>the second number. The symbol for this is <.

Chapter 12. Conic sections

a. -equivalence
c. Undefined
b. Less than12
d. Undefined

21. <U>A <U>vertical line </U>goes up and down or from North to South.</U>
a. Vertical line12
c. Undefined
b. -equivalence
d. Undefined

22. If one number is to the right of another number on the number line, this number is <U>greater than </U>the number on the left. The symbol that is used is >.
a. -equivalence
c. Undefined
b. Greater than12
d. Undefined

23. The _____ or central tendency of a list of n numbers. All the values are added together and then divided by the number of values. It is also call the mean..
a. ADE classification
c. Undefined
b. Average12
d. Undefined

24. A <U>quadratic</U> contains at least one squared term.
a. Quadratic12
c. Undefined
b. -equivalence
d. Undefined

25. A <U>quadratic equation </U>is written in standard form as ax²+ bx + c = 0. In general, a _____ must contain a squared term.
a. Quadratic equation12
c. Undefined
b. -equivalence
d. Undefined

26. An _____ combines numbers, operators, and/or variables but contains no equal or inequality sign.
a. Expression12
c. Undefined
b. ADE classification
d. Undefined

27. _____ (or summation) is one of the basic operations of arithmetic. In its simplest form, _____ combines two numbers, the augend and addend, into a single number, the sum.
a. ADE classification
c. Undefined
b. Addition12
d. Undefined

28. A _____ is a well-defined collection of objects considered as a whole.
a. Set12
c. Undefined
b. -equivalence
d. Undefined

29. A set of numbers that satisfies a given equation or inequality is a _____.
a. Solution set12
c. Undefined
b. -equivalence
d. Undefined

Chapter 1

1. b	2. a	3. a	4. b	5. b	6. a	7. a	8. a	9. b	10. b
11. a	12. a	13. a	14. b	15. a	16. b	17. b	18. a	19. b	20. a
21. a	22. b	23. b	24. b	25. a	26. a	27. b	28. a	29. b	30. a
31. b	32. a	33. a	34. b	35. b	36. a	37. b	38. b	39. b	40. b
41. a	42. b	43. b	44. b	45. b	46. a	47. a	48. b	49. a	50. b
51. b	52. a	53. a	54. b	55. a	56. b	57. a	58. a	59. b	60. b
61. a	62. b	63. a	64. b	65. b	66. a	67. a	68. a	69. b	70. b
71. a	72. a	73. a	74. a	75. a	76. b	77. b	78. b	79. a	80. b
81. a	82. a	83. a	84. b	85. b	86. a	87. b	88. a	89. a	90. a
91. a	92. b	93. a	94. a	95. b	96. b	97. a	98. b	99. a	100. a
101. a	102. b	103. a	104. b	105. a	106. a	107. b	108. a	109. b	110. b
111. b	112. a	113. a	114. b	115. a	116. b	117. b	118. a	119. a	120. a
121. a	122. b	123. b	124. a	125. b	126. b	127. a	128. a	129. a	130. a
131. b									

Chapter 2

1. b	2. a	3. b	4. b	5. b	6. a	7. a	8. b	9. a	10. a
11. a	12. a	13. b	14. a	15. b	16. b	17. b	18. b	19. b	20. a
21. a	22. b	23. a	24. a	25. a	26. b	27. a	28. b	29. a	30. a
31. b	32. a	33. a	34. a	35. b	36. a	37. b	38. a	39. b	40. b
41. b	42. b	43. a	44. a	45. a	46. a	47. b	48. a	49. b	50. b
51. a	52. b	53. a	54. b	55. a	56. a	57. a	58. b	59. a	60. a
61. b	62. b	63. a	64. a	65. b	66. b	67. b	68. b	69. a	70. a
71. a	72. b	73. b	74. a	75. a	76. a	77. b	78. a	79. b	80. a
81. b	82. b	83. b	84. b	85. a	86. a	87. b	88. a	89. b	90. b
91. b	92. a	93. b	94. b	95. a	96. a	97. a	98. a	99. b	100. b
101. b	102. b	103. b	104. a	105. b	106. b	107. a	108. b	109. b	110. a
111. b	112. a	113. a	114. a	115. b	116. a	117. a	118. b	119. b	120. a
121. a	122. a	123. a	124. b	125. b	126. b				

ANSWER KEY

Chapter 3

1. a	2. b	3. b	4. b	5. a	6. b	7. a	8. b	9. b	10. b
11. a	12. b	13. a	14. b	15. b	16. b	17. a	18. a	19. b	20. b
21. b	22. b	23. b	24. b	25. a	26. b	27. a	28. b	29. a	30. a
31. b	32. a	33. b	34. b	35. a	36. b	37. b	38. a	39. a	40. b
41. b	42. a	43. a	44. b	45. a	46. a	47. a	48. b	49. b	50. b
51. a	52. b	53. b	54. b	55. a	56. a	57. a	58. b	59. a	60. b
61. b	62. a	63. b	64. a	65. a	66. b	67. a	68. a	69. b	70. a
71. b	72. b	73. a	74. b	75. b	76. a	77. a	78. b	79. a	80. a
81. a	82. a	83. b	84. b	85. b	86. a	87. a	88. a	89. a	90. a
91. b	92. a	93. b	94. a	95. b	96. a	97. a	98. b	99. b	100. a
101. b	102. b	103. a	104. b	105. a	106. a	107. a	108. a	109. a	110. b
111. a	112. b	113. a	114. a	115. a	116. a	117. b	118. b	119. a	120. a
121. a	122. a	123. b	124. b	125. b	126. b	127. a	128. b	129. a	130. a
131. b	132. b	133. a	134. a	135. a	136. b	137. a	138. b	139. a	140. b
141. a	142. b	143. a	144. b	145. a	146. a	147. a	148. a	149. a	150. b
151. a	152. a	153. b							

Chapter 4

1. a	2. a	3. a	4. a	5. a	6. a	7. b	8. a	9. b	10. a
11. a	12. b	13. a	14. b	15. b	16. b	17. a	18. a	19. a	20. a
21. b	22. b	23. b	24. b	25. b	26. a	27. b	28. b	29. a	30. a
31. b	32. a	33. b	34. a	35. a	36. a	37. a	38. a	39. a	40. a
41. a	42. a	43. a	44. a	45. a	46. a	47. b	48. a	49. a	50. b
51. a	52. b	53. a	54. a	55. a	56. b	57. b	58. b	59. b	60. a
61. a	62. a	63. b	64. b	65. b	66. a	67. b	68. a	69. b	70. a
71. a	72. a	73. b	74. b	75. a	76. b	77. a	78. b	79. b	80. a
81. a	82. b	83. a	84. b	85. b	86. b	87. a	88. a	89. b	90. a
91. a	92. a	93. b	94. a	95. b	96. a	97. a	98. a	99. b	100. a
101. b	102. b	103. a	104. a	105. b	106. b	107. a	108. b		

Chapter 5

1. b	2. b	3. b	4. b	5. a	6. b	7. b	8. b	9. a	10. b
11. a	12. a	13. b	14. a	15. a	16. a	17. a	18. b	19. a	20. b
21. b	22. a	23. a	24. a	25. a	26. a	27. b	28. b	29. b	30. a
31. b	32. b	33. a	34. b	35. a	36. a	37. b	38. b	39. b	40. b
41. b	42. b	43. b	44. a	45. a	46. a	47. a	48. b	49. a	50. b
51. b	52. a	53. a	54. a	55. a	56. b	57. a	58. b	59. b	60. b
61. b	62. b	63. b	64. a	65. a	66. b	67. b	68. b	69. b	70. b
71. a	72. a	73. a	74. a	75. a	76. a	77. b	78. b	79. b	80. a
81. b	82. a	83. a	84. a	85. b	86. a	87. a	88. b	89. b	90. a
91. b	92. b	93. b	94. a	95. b	96. b	97. a	98. a	99. b	100. b
101. a	102. a	103. a	104. b	105. a	106. a	107. b	108. a	109. a	110. b
111. a	112. b	113. a	114. a	115. a	116. a	117. b	118. b	119. a	120. a
121. a	122. a	123. b	124. b	125. a	126. a	127. b	128. b	129. b	130. b
131. b	132. b	133. a	134. b	135. a	136. a	137. b	138. a	139. a	140. b
141. b	142. a	143. b	144. b	145. a	146. a	147. a	148. a	149. b	150. a
151. b	152. a	153. a	154. b	155. a	156. a	157. a	158. a	159. b	160. b
161. a	162. b	163. b	164. a	165. b					

Chapter 6

1. b	2. b	3. b	4. b	5. b	6. b	7. a	8. b	9. a	10. a
11. a	12. b	13. b	14. b	15. a	16. b	17. a	18. b	19. b	20. a
21. a	22. b	23. b	24. b	25. b	26. a	27. a	28. b	29. a	30. a
31. a	32. a	33. a	34. b	35. a	36. a	37. a	38. a	39. a	40. a
41. b	42. a	43. b	44. b	45. b	46. a	47. b	48. a	49. b	50. a
51. b	52. b	53. b	54. b	55. a	56. a	57. b	58. b	59. a	60. a
61. a	62. b	63. a	64. a	65. b	66. b	67. b	68. b	69. a	70. a
71. b	72. a	73. a	74. a	75. a	76. b	77. a	78. b	79. b	80. a
81. a	82. b	83. a	84. a	85. a	86. b	87. a	88. a	89. b	90. b
91. a	92. a	93. b	94. a	95. b	96. a	97. a	98. a	99. b	100. b
101. a	102. b	103. a	104. a	105. b	106. b	107. a	108. a	109. a	110. a
111. b	112. a	113. a	114. b	115. a	116. b	117. b	118. a	119. a	120. b
121. b	122. a	123. a	124. a	125. b	126. a	127. a	128. b	129. a	130. a
131. a	132. a	133. b	134. a	135. a					

ANSWER KEY

Chapter 7

1. a	2. b	3. b	4. a	5. b	6. a	7. a	8. a	9. b	10. a
11. b	12. b	13. b	14. b	15. a	16. b	17. b	18. b	19. b	20. a
21. a	22. a	23. a	24. b	25. a	26. a	27. a	28. a	29. a	30. b
31. b	32. b	33. a	34. a	35. b	36. b	37. b	38. b	39. a	40. b
41. b	42. a	43. b	44. a	45. a	46. a	47. b	48. b	49. b	50. b
51. a	52. a	53. a	54. a	55. a	56. b	57. a	58. b	59. b	60. a
61. b	62. a	63. b	64. a	65. b	66. b	67. b	68. b	69. b	70. a
71. a	72. b	73. a	74. a	75. a	76. a	77. a	78. b	79. a	80. a
81. b	82. a	83. a	84. b	85. a	86. b	87. b	88. b	89. a	90. b
91. b	92. b	93. a	94. a	95. b	96. b	97. a	98. a	99. a	100. b
101. a	102. b	103. b	104. a	105. b	106. b	107. b	108. b	109. b	110. b
111. a	112. a	113. b	114. a	115. a	116. b	117. b	118. b	119. b	120. b
121. b	122. b	123. a	124. b	125. a	126. a	127. b	128. b	129. b	130. a
131. b									

Chapter 8

1. b	2. b	3. a	4. b	5. a	6. a	7. a	8. a	9. b	10. b
11. a	12. a	13. b	14. a	15. b	16. a	17. a	18. b	19. a	20. b
21. a	22. a	23. b	24. b	25. b	26. b	27. b	28. a	29. a	30. a
31. b	32. a	33. b	34. b	35. b	36. b	37. a	38. b	39. b	40. b
41. a	42. b	43. b	44. b	45. a	46. a	47. b	48. b	49. b	50. b
51. a	52. a	53. a	54. a	55. b	56. b	57. b	58. b	59. b	60. a
61. a	62. b	63. a	64. b	65. a	66. a	67. a	68. b	69. b	70. b
71. b	72. a	73. a	74. a	75. a	76. a	77. a	78. b	79. b	80. a
81. a	82. a	83. a	84. b	85. a	86. a	87. a	88. a	89. b	90. b
91. a	92. a	93. a	94. a	95. b	96. b	97. a	98. a	99. b	100. a
101. b	102. a	103. b	104. a	105. a	106. a	107. a	108. a	109. b	110. a
111. b	112. b	113. a	114. b	115. b	116. a	117. a	118. b	119. a	120. b
121. b	122. a	123. b	124. a	125. a	126. b	127. a	128. a	129. b	130. a
131. b	132. b	133. a	134. b	135. b	136. a	137. a	138. b	139. b	140. b
141. b	142. b	143. a							

Chapter 9

1. b	2. b	3. b	4. b	5. b	6. a	7. a	8. b	9. a	10. a
11. b	12. a	13. b	14. b	15. a	16. b	17. a	18. b	19. b	20. a
21. a	22. a	23. a	24. a	25. a	26. b	27. b	28. b	29. a	30. a
31. a	32. a	33. a	34. b	35. b	36. a	37. a	38. a	39. b	40. b
41. b	42. a	43. b	44. a	45. a	46. a	47. a	48. a	49. a	50. b
51. a	52. b	53. a	54. a	55. a	56. a	57. a	58. b	59. b	60. a
61. a	62. b	63. a	64. b	65. a	66. b	67. b	68. b	69. a	70. b
71. a	72. b	73. b	74. b	75. b	76. b	77. a	78. a	79. b	80. b
81. a	82. a	83. a	84. a	85. b	86. a	87. b	88. b		

Chapter 10

1. a	2. b	3. a	4. a	5. b	6. a	7. a	8. a	9. a	10. a
11. a	12. b	13. a	14. b	15. a	16. a	17. a	18. a	19. b	20. b
21. a	22. b	23. a	24. b	25. a	26. a	27. b	28. a	29. b	30. a
31. b	32. a	33. a	34. b	35. a	36. a	37. b	38. b	39. b	40. b
41. b	42. b								

Chapter 11

1. b	2. b	3. b	4. a	5. a	6. a	7. a	8. a	9. a	10. b
11. b	12. a	13. a	14. a	15. b	16. b	17. a	18. b	19. b	20. a
21. a	22. b	23. b	24. a	25. a	26. b	27. b	28. a	29. a	30. a
31. b	32. a	33. b	34. b	35. a	36. b	37. a	38. a	39. a	40. b
41. b	42. b	43. a	44. b						

Chapter 12

1. b	2. b	3. b	4. a	5. b	6. a	7. b	8. a	9. b	10. a
11. b	12. a	13. a	14. b	15. a	16. a	17. b	18. a	19. b	20. b
21. a	22. b	23. b	24. a	25. a	26. a	27. b	28. a	29. a	